# Developing Infill Housing in Inner-City Neighborhoods
## Opportunities and Strategies

**Diane R. Suchman**

*with*

**Margaret B. Sowell**

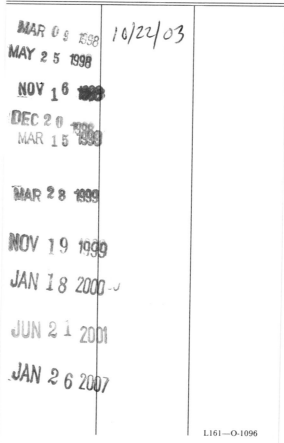

**Urban Land
Institute**

## ULI–the Urban Land Institute

ULI–the Urban Land Institute is a nonprofit education and research institute that is supported and directed by its members. Its mission is to provide responsible leadership in the use of land in order to enhance the total environment.

ULI sponsors educational programs and forums to encourage an open international exchange of ideas and sharing of experience; initiates research that anticipates emerging land use trends and issues and proposes creative solutions based on this research; provides advisory services; and publishes a wide variety of materials to disseminate information on land use and development.

Established in 1936, the Institute today has more than 13,000 members and associates from approximately 50 countries representing the entire spectrum of the land use and development disciplines. They include developers, builders, property owners, investors, architects, public officials, planners, real estate brokers, appraisers, attorneys, engineers, financiers, academics, students, and librarians. ULI members contribute to higher standards of land use by sharing their knowledge and experience. The Institute has long been recognized as one of America's most respected and widely quoted sources of objective information on urban planning, growth, and development.

**Richard M. Rosan**
Executive Vice President

## ULI Project Staff

Rachelle L. Levitt
*Senior Vice President, Policy and Practice*

Lloyd W. Bookout
*Vice President, Real Estate Practice*

Nancy S. Stewart
*Director, Book Program*

Helene Y. Redmond, HYR Graphics
*Layout/Book Design*

Ann Lenney
*Copy Editor*

Betsy VanBuskirk
*Cover Design*

Diann Stanley-Austin
*Production Manager*

Cover Photograph: Crawford Square, Pittsburgh, Pennsylvania; photograph courtesy of UDA Architects

Recommended bibliographic listing:
Suchman, Diane R. *Developing Infill Housing in Inner-City Neighborhoods: Opportunities and Strategies.* Washington, D.C.: ULI–the Urban Land Institute, 1997.

ULI Catalog Number: D15
International Standard Book Number: 0-87420-818-1
Library of Congress Catalog Card Number: 97-61907

Copyright 1997 by ULI–the Urban Land Institute
1025 Thomas Jefferson Street, N.W.
Suite 500 West
Washington, D.C. 20007-5201

## ULI Advisory Committee

## About the Authors

### Diane R. Suchman

Diane R. Suchman is an independent researcher, writer, and consultant specializing in housing, community development, and revitalization strategies for low-income neighborhoods. She recently served as special assistant to HUD's Secretary for Policy Development and Research. Previously, Suchman was the director of housing and community development research for the Urban Land Institute. She is the author of three books, including *Public/Private Housing Partnerships* and *Revitalizing Low-Income Neighborhoods*, and numerous articles, papers, book chapters, and case studies. She has also worked as a real estate market analyst.

### Margaret B. Sowell

Margaret B. Sowell, president of Real Estate Strategies, Inc., has 27 years of experience with real estate and economic development, as a government official, private developer, and adviser to public agencies and private companies. Sowell worked with the U.S. Department of Housing and Urban Development for 15 years. As a private sector developer, she has had experience with a Wilmington, Delaware, development company. A real estate consultant since 1986, Sowell has assisted with affordable housing developments in a number of cities. She has prepared market and financial analyses for public and private sector clients and has assisted in structuring public/private financing packages. Sowell is a trustee of the Urban Land Institute.

## Acknowledgments

This book is the work of many hands. I would like to thank Meg Sowell, Tom Safran, Frank Martin, Barbara Udell, Barry Humphries, Donald Carter, Patricia Burke, Jon Welhoefer, Joe Corcoran, and Hillary Zimmerman for taking time to review preliminary materials, offer advice, and suggest resources. I am indebted to the Local Government Commission of Sacramento, California, for sending case study examples illustrating ways in which public agencies can encourage infill development, and for generously sharing their previously published materials on this subject. Thanks also to Susan Hobart and Robert Schwartz, formerly with Heartland Properties, Inc., who wrote the text on low-income housing tax credits in the financing chapter. The developers whose projects are featured in this book and members of their staffs all responded promptly and enthusiastically to my inquiries and requests for information.

The book's production crew, especially Nancy Stewart, Ann Lenney, Diann Stanley-Austin, and Helene Redmond, were outstanding. And finally, I would like to thank Rachelle Levitt and the many people on ULI's research staff including Bob Dunphy, Dean Schwanke, Gayle Berens, Joan Campbell, Mary Schwartz, and, most of all, Lloyd Bookout, for their cheerful, ever-ready advice and assistance.

**Diane R. Suchman**

# Contents

## Chapter Four. Mixed-Income Housing 59

Market Considerations, 60 ▪ Development Process, 61 ▪ Transformation of Public Housing into Mixed-Income Communities, 64

*Project Profiles:* Westminster Place, 72 ▪ Del Norte Place, 74 ▪ Homan Square, 77

## Chapter Five. Public/Private Financing 83

Public/Private Partnerships, 84 ▪ The Federal Low-Income Housing Tax Credit, 87 ▪ Tax-Exempt Bonds, 91 ▪ Putting the Pieces Together, 93 ▪ The Developer's Return, 94

*Project Profiles:* Wells Court Apartments, Strathern Park, Maple Court, Meacham Park

## Chapter Six. How Local Governments Can Help 105

Ten Suggested Measures, 105 ▪ Conclusion, 112

*Project Profiles:* Quality Hill, 113 ▪ Trinity Court, 117 ▪ South Williamsburg Homes, 120

# Foreword

ULI's long-term commitment to research, education, and advisory services related to affordable housing and inner-city revitalization issues has taken many forms over the years. This commitment became more formalized in 1987, when the trustees of ULI–the Urban Land Institute, concerned about the increasing shortage of affordable housing, created and funded the Low- and Moderate-Income Housing Task Force to consider strategies and disseminate information that would help solve this problem. This task force—chaired by ULI trustees Leanne Lachman and Nina Gruen and staffed by Diane Suchman—initiated a four-year research and education effort that resulted in numerous books, professional development seminars, articles, case studies, and advisory services panels. The success of the Low- and Moderate-Income Housing Task Force illustrated the positive influence that ULI could exert on this important real estate–based social issue.

ULI expanded its scope of interest in affordable housing and inner-city revitalization issues in 1990 with the creation of the Inner-City Community Building (ICCB) program. The ICCB program was launched to involve the private sector more extensively in inner-city issues and to bring the resources of ULI's membership to bear on urban problems. The ICCB program today offers direct technical assistance to inner-city communities and provides education and research projects that are designed to attract ULI members and their colleagues to the opportunities that exist— or can be created—in established urban areas.

This book builds on ULI's past programs and activities. In particular, ULI's research committee in 1995 supported the development of a series of five affordable housing working papers to explore a variety of specific techniques that might offer realistic, workable solutions: 1) *Financing Multi-family Housing Using Section 42 Low-Income Housing Tax Credits;* 2) *Manufactured Housing: An Affordable Alternative;* 3) *Mixed-Income Housing;* 4) *Transformation of Public Housing to Mixed-Income Communities;* and 5) *Infill Housing: Opportunities and Strategies for Inner-City Neighborhoods.* The research conducted for these papers provided invaluable background for this book. In addition, the Developing Infill Housing symposium, held in Milwaukee in September 1995 and cosponsored by ULI and the city of Milwaukee, helped to lay the groundwork for the strategies and project examples featured in this publication.

By compiling in one volume much of ULI's research findings over the past years on successful strategies for developing infill housing, ULI hopes to inform public, private, and nonprofit organizations about current best practices and policy initiatives. Inner-city neighborhoods across the United States are rich in diversity, architecture, and culture. They also contain great stores of often underused physical infrastructure. The reintroduction of affordable, contextually designed housing to these neighborhoods is pivotal to the long-term health not only of our inner-city neighborhoods and future generations of residents, but also of our cities.

**Lloyd W. Bookout**

## CHAPTER 1

# Urban Change and Infill Development

In many cities across the United States, once-vibrant neighborhoods are pocked by parcels of vacant land that have been bypassed by earlier development, or are left with structures that have deteriorated or been torn down. Local governments are often eager to see such land redeveloped. And, especially where the demand for housing is strong, developers are looking to use infill sites to create housing that appeals to a diverse housing market, including downtown workers.

This book is intended to provide developers and city officials with an overview of the opportunities and challenges of developing infill housing in transitional or distressed urban residential neighborhoods, and with some strategies for pursuing such developments.

Chapter 1 surveys the changes that have taken place in America's cities and places the discussion of infill housing development in city neighborhoods within the larger context of the physical, economic, political, and social dynamics that are shaping metropolitan areas. In Chapter 2, the authors outline the process for analyzing inner-city housing markets, highlighting the differences between older urban neighborhood environments and new suburban locations. Development considerations are the subject of Chapter 3; included are site selection, neighborhood issues, project conceptualization and design, and community relations. Chapter 4 focuses on mixed-income developments, often preferred in inner cities as a means of attracting and serving a more diverse population; this discussion involves a section on transforming distressed public housing developments into mixed-income communities. Chapter 5 summarizes financing sources and approaches to housing development, while Chapter 6 covers the array of tools that cities can use to encourage infill housing development. Many project examples appear throughout the book, to illustrate the wide range of housing types and development approaches that have succeeded in urban infill locations.

## Forces Changing America's Cities

Changes in the economics, demographics, and land use patterns of America's cities have drained the vitality from many urban neighborhoods. America's metropolitan areas differ from one another in many important ways: in economic base, physical character, population characteristics and distribution, and the direction and rate of change. Thus, generalizations are difficult. However, a number of forces are affecting all metropolitan regions, and certain patterns of urban change are clear. Economic restructuring from manufacturing to service and knowledge-based industries, the global nature of modern economic activity, the dizzying pace of technological change, the rise in immigration, shortages of labor, the aging of the world's population, the growth in environmental awareness, and changing patterns of governmental funding have all affected the character and fortunes of metropolitan areas.

The shift to a postindustrial, service-oriented economy has had a complex effect on patterns of urbanization. Loss of manufacturing industries in many cities has caused a concomitant loss of low-skill jobs that have paid well. At the same time, the rise of technical and service-oriented industries has created a demand for knowledge-based and service workers. Globalization of the economy has stimulated greater business mobility, efficiency, and flexibility. As a result, metropolitan areas must now compete as economic regions.

Economic and technological changes have also helped transform land use patterns in metropolitan areas. The most profound land use change during the second half of this century has been the suburbanization of population and jobs. Rapid technological change has opened new vistas of creativity and given people and businesses more freedom of movement. Advances in communications have enabled companies to relocate their back-office functions and, in some cases, their headquarters to suburban or even rural areas.

Many observers believe that suburbanization has also been driven by public policies and by actions that have encouraged families to locate in or relocate to the suburbs, drawing middle-class housing consumers away from city neighborhoods. Motivated by sustained economic growth; low-cost, federally insured home mortgages; cheap land; the availability of automobiles and low-cost gasoline; the construction of federally subsidized highways; and a strong cultural preference for single-family houses on large lots, most people who have a choice have chosen to live in the suburbs rather than the cities.

As a result of this outmigration, within America's 522 central cities, population density has declined by 50 percent since 1950. (The most obvious exceptions are the few cities that have experienced significant immigration from other countries.) As of 1990, almost 80 percent of the nation's population lived in the suburbs. Jobs have followed people. Today, 80 percent of new office construction is taking place in the suburbs, and in many metropolitan areas, suburbs account for the majority of office space. A recent survey by the National Association of Home Builders (NAHB) confirms this trend, finding that eight of ten homebuyers will choose a traditional single-family house in an outlying suburb over a similarly priced but smaller townhouse located close to the city.

Because of a number of factors—including the declining availability of well-paying low-skill jobs, inadequate educational preparation for knowledge-based or technical employment,

higher home prices in the suburbs, and continuing racial barriers to economic advancement and housing opportunity—many lower-income African American households have remained in central cities. Numerous studies document the rising incidence, concentration, and persistence of poverty, particularly among African Americans, in the low-income neighborhoods of many cities over the past 25 years.

Immigration, especially from Latin America and Asia, has increased the proportion and diversity of minorities in the population and has changed cities' demographic profiles. Most minority growth has been concentrated in the South and West and in certain metropolitan areas. Twenty percent of total minority growth during the 1980s was in Los Angeles; half of all minority growth in the 1980s was in nine metropolitan areas. (More than two-thirds of all metropolitan areas have less than the average percentage of minorities.)

Within metropolitan areas, immigrants and minorities tend to be concentrated in the urban cores. As of 1990, many central cities had "minority majorities," including Chicago (62.4 percent minority); Dallas (53.1 percent minority); Detroit (79.7 percent minority); Los Angeles (54.2 percent minority); and Washington, D.C. (73.5 percent minority).[1]

Change has also occurred in the age distribution of the population. With the aging of the baby boomers, the nation's population is growing older. In addition, the numbers, proportion, and rate of increase of the elderly population have climbed. In 1900, 4 percent of America's population was over 65; in 1990, 13 percent. Cities tend to house larger proportions of elderly residents than the suburbs, which is an economically significant factor because elderly people tend to have lower earned incomes but to generate disproportionate demand for social services—especially health care.

## Effects on Cities

Not all cities are alike. Some have succeeded in restructuring their economies successfully and rebuilding their downtowns. Others have not. The pattern of population loss is also not uniform. Of 18 central cities that lost population during the 1970s, six gained population during the 1980s. All but one of the remainder slowed the rate of population loss. Cities that serve as headquarters of corporations and related finance, insurance, and real estate (FIRE) industries tended to grow in

population and employment. Port-of-entry cities such as Los Angeles, San Francisco, New York, and Miami also grew.[2]

How cities have fared during this period of change has depended on the quality of local leadership; the nature of local labor markets; patterns of income and poverty; whether these cities are elastic or inelastic (i.e., whether they have the power to annex); their nature as old industrial cities or newer, more diversified, automobile-oriented ones; gain or loss of population; and other factors. And the trends noted above have affected different cities differently. The fortunes of individual cities dependent on specific industries—such as oil, the military/industrial complex, or tourism—have risen or fallen with those industries. Some cities, such as Youngstown, Newark, Cleveland, Pittsburgh, and the Bronx and Brooklyn boroughs of New York City, had declined but are now rebounding.

## Impacts on Inner-City Neighborhoods

Today, central cities' demographic profiles differ sharply from those of the suburbs. As middle-income families have moved out of the cities and into the suburbs, poor residents have been left behind and joined by recent immigrants. Cities have become more racially diverse, contain more young adults and elderly people as a percentage

of the population, and show a greater incidence and concentration of poverty than do suburban jurisdictions. As a result, racial and economic disparities between cities and suburbs have widened, and there is a spatial mismatch between jobs and housing and a fiscal mismatch between the location of higher-income populations and revenue needs.

In addition, central cities are plagued by two issues that make central-city neighborhoods difficult places in which to live and raise children and that thus deter investment in the local housing market: (1) urban school systems, which are perceived as ineffective (and even unsafe) warehouses of poorly educated, disadvantaged, and minority students; and (2) distressed neighborhoods, which exhibit the full range of social problems associated with concentrated poverty—particularly crime, drugs, gangs, and long-term unemployment.

These factors, which discourage middle-class households from locating in inner-city neighborhoods, along with projected lower future demand for housing overall, could cause more problems for central cities if unrestrained housing development in suburbs continues.

The continuing deterioration of many city neighborhoods should be a matter of concern to all metropolitan-area residents, regardless of where they live. The presence of blighted areas in the core cities of the nation creates a sense of physical decay, economic drain, and spiritual degra-

dation among people of the city, the region,
and the nation.

## Why Should Suburbanites Care about Central Cities?

Although the value of central cities is difficult to
quantify, it is clear that they possess considerable
value that extends beyond their jurisdictional
boundaries. Cities remain the symbolic, social,
and economic hearts of their metropolitan regions. Mention the name of a metropolitan area,
and the image that springs to mind is not that of
a suburban office center but that of the downtown. The city is the real and symbolic center of
the region, the physical embodiment of the city's

history, character, and business reputation. And
this center can be a source of civic pride or of
embarrassment to all area citizens.

A city typically contains a one-of-a-kind amen-
ity, such as a historic area, cultural complex, or
waterfront, that is highly valued by the entire region and sometimes by the nation. For example,
Riverwalk in San Antonio, the French Quarter in
New Orleans, the Mall of monuments in Washington, D.C., Lincoln Center or Central Park in New
York, Chicago's Miracle Mile, and the Golden
Gate Bridge in San Francisco are amenities of
national significance.

Central cities tend to perform specific functions
well. They are the locations of choice for activities that benefit from face-to-face communication
among the city's public and private leadership.
The high density of cities enables decisionmakers
to gather and share information, skills, products,
and services. As a result, "many of the great inno-
vations of the U.S. economy have been incubated
in the nation's cities."[3] Some have argued that advancing technology has made face-to-face contact unimportant, yet electronic communication
"cannot be randomized or accidental in the same
way as meetings at offices, restaurants, churches,
or just [in] the street. Nor can electronic meetings convey the same completeness of meaning
as face-to-face contacts . . . and electronic contacts cannot be entirely entrusted with the confi-
dential communication so important in politics
and government affairs."[4]

In addition, cities "have unique agglomeration economies that define an important and specialized role for the central city and the region."[5] "Dense urban environments can lead to unexpected combinations of seemingly unrelated ideas that may provide important leaps forward in knowledge."[6] And central cities are the hubs of region-serving networks such as sewage purification systems, electrical power grids, telephone networks, water supply systems, water ports, railroads, trucking centers, and so forth.[7]

Within the historic central city stand the architecturally distinctive buildings, monuments, and plazas that evoke a city's unique history and character. Cities often contain governmental complexes, great universities, convention centers, museums, hospital centers, libraries, festival marketplaces, zoos, performing arts centers, research institutions, and sports facilities that serve the entire region, offering a wide range of cultural events, civic activities, educational opportunities, entertainment, and recreational opportunities. A recent survey of residents of the 100 largest American cities revealed that among residents of the suburbs, half of the families surveyed had included at least one family member who worked in the central city; 67 percent depended on the central city for major medical care; and 43 percent had a family member attending or planning to attend a central city–based institution of higher learning.[8]

Central cities are also important to the regional economy and its ability to compete in the global marketplace. Cities are labor markets where people seek work and where companies seek workers. Because of their locations and critical mass, central cities are fertile environments for firms and individuals offering a high degree of specialization in expertise and services. Companies located in suburban jurisdictions often depend on central-city suppliers for various corporate services, and many highly paid suburbanites work in the central city. In fact, wages for central-city jobs are on average 20 percent higher than for suburban jobs, though many of these high-paying jobs are held by suburbanites.[9] Cities have also traditionally served as "zones of emergence" for the poor, for racial and ethnic minorities, and for immigrants.[10]

A number of studies have indicated that the fortunes of central cities and their suburbs move in concert. Where cities tend to be strong and productive, suburban prosperity is greater. There is a direct correlation between city/suburban disparity and economic growth. Where disparities are great, economic growth is slower. And population change in central cities is related to suburban population growth; cities with high rates of population loss have declining or slower-growing suburbs. In short, cities (and suburbs) have come to be recognized as parts of a larger, regional economic unit that cannot be easily defined or divided along traditional jurisdictional lines.[11]

From a physical standpoint, central cities represent substantial public and private investment in the built environment (infrastructure, buildings, and the like). Allowing that physical investment to deteriorate, and with it the social fabric of the community, is wasteful and threatens not only the quality of life of city residents but also the vitality of nearby areas and ultimately of the entire region, where such deterioration can easily spread.

And finally, most people *like* cities, at least cities the way they were before concentrations of poverty threatened their social stability. Across the country, architects, urban designers, and developers are at work creating "neotraditional" communities in suburban, urban, and resort locations that have been designed with many of the same elements that characterize older city neighborhoods: public gathering spaces; houses that front on the street; pedestrian-friendly distances to shopping, recreation, and civic activity; narrow, grid-patterned streets; and similar characteristics. Such developments respond to a nostalgia within a portion of the housing market for the city life of yesteryear, and to a desire among these same homebuyers for a more urban lifestyle. These physical conditions exist—or can be recreated—in city neighborhoods.

In the words of ULI Trustee Anthony Downs, "The belief among suburbanites that they are independent of central cities is a delusion. So is the belief that central cities are obsolete. . . . Both fallacies have consequences dangerous to America's economic and social health."[12]

## Rebuilding the City

Recreating vibrant central cities will require a multipronged strategy that includes redefining the functions of the metropolitan core consistent with global economic realities, metropolitan land use patterns, and continuing advances in technology. It will involve building a new economic base consistent with those redefined functions, ensuring accessibility from within and beyond the city core, finding productive ways to reuse obsolete buildings (especially by rehabilitating architecturally and historically significant structures),

Del Norte Place is a vital new presence along San Pablo Boulevard, the main street of El Cerrito, California. The development provides high-density, transit-oriented housing on an infill site.

and creating inviting environments in which people can gather. And it will involve making cities more livable by revitalizing and attracting a more diverse population to the deteriorated older neighborhoods near the central business district and inner suburbs.

This book proceeds on the assumption that a major reason why most middle-class people choose homes in suburban locations is that attractive alternatives—affordable, well-designed homes with the desired amenities and services in safe, well-kept neighborhoods with convenient shopping, good schools, and good public services —do not exist in many central cities.

Revitalizing neighborhoods and creating new housing opportunities in central cities can be achieved through a number of different approaches used in combination. Many cities, such as Milwaukee, Chicago, and Washington, D.C., have aggressively promoted downtown housing by encouraging the construction of luxury rental apartments and condominiums in the downtown. In some cities, such as New York and Denver, existing vacant, underused, or obsolete buildings are being transformed into rental apartments. Other cities, such as Pittsburgh and Memphis, contain large tracts of underused land near the downtown core that are being developed as new communities. And in other areas, like Atlanta, St. Louis, and San Francisco, distressed public housing developments

are being demolished or rehabilitated and rebuilt as mixed-income communities.[13] Many of these approaches involve the revitalization of inner-city neighborhoods through privately developed infill housing projects.

## Why Promote Infill Development?

Vacant properties amid city neighborhoods weaken those communities. They bespeak physical, economic, and social deterioration and are susceptible to graffiti, arson, the accumulation of trash, and other problems that reduce the value of surrounding properties and affect the success of nearby businesses. Taken together, "the cost of supporting abandoned areas acts as a monumental social and economic drag on regional economies and the state and country as a whole."[14]

Development of infill sites in established city neighborhoods can provide many public benefits. It can furnish needed housing, expand opportunities for homeownership, and, thus help retain and attract back to the city much-valued middle-income taxpayers. Infill development can enable local governments to privatize their inventories of publicly owned properties and to put vacant land and buildings back on the tax rolls. Development of infill parcels can also help rebuild the city fabric, eliminate existing and potential neighborhood eyesores, and fuel additional investment and economic activity within the community. Particularly when it involves rehabilitation of older buildings, infill development can help preserve the existing housing stock and historic structures and help retain the community's character and cultural heritage.

As part of a regional strategy to accommodate population growth, wise reuse of infill parcels can minimize the consumption of agricultural land at the urban fringe and reduce the need for long commutes, automobile use, and fuel consumption by creating housing close to the central city and to public transit.

Interest in infill development has been spurred by diminishing local government budgets, which have sparked interest in development opportunities that do not require substantial public expenditure. For example, developments that maximize the use of existing infrastructure and transportation facilities, rather than require new ones, can avoid the capital costs of new infrastructure construction and can help spread among more users the fixed costs of operating and maintaining the existing infrastructure.[15]

## Types of Infill Housing Developments

As illustrated by the following project examples and others interspersed throughout the book, infill housing developments can take many forms, depending on the dynamics of the market, the amount and configuration of land (or structures) available, and the character and history of the immediate area. Infill projects can include single-family houses on small lots, townhouses, rental apartments, condominiums, and cooperatives. Houses can be stick-built, manufactured or modular units, rehabilitated older structures or historic buildings, or any combination of these. The target market can be all low-income households, households that represent a range of incomes, or all households that can pay market-rate rents or sales prices. For example:

- In Seattle, Kucher/Rutherford, the developer of Pine Street Cottages, renovated ten one-bedroom cottages on a one-third-acre site as affordable condominiums for first-time buyers.
- In Pittsburgh, McCormack Baron & Associates is developing Crawford Square, a mixed-income residential development in the Lower Hill dis-

McCormack Baron & Associates is building Crawford Square, a mixed-income residential project in Pittsburgh's Lower Hill district, in cooperation with community development corporations, the city's urban redevelopment authority, and the state and federal governments.

# The Relationship between Infill Housing and Transportation Planning

Infill development offers significant transportation advantages, a key reason why it is desired by transit agencies and preferred by regional transportation organizations. It offers no-cost growth for the transit market and also smart growth for highways because residents in established communities do not have to drive as much as suburbanites to satisfy their daily travel needs.

A significant challenge to transit agencies is that their prime market, city residents traveling in and around town, is declining. The 1990 Census reported that workers living and working in the cities accounted for a mere 10 percent of the growth in the U.S. commuting market since 1980, with many of those workers living in smaller regions not well served by transit. The primary growth market in travel consists of suburban residents traveling to suburban destinations, who represent 58 percent of the growth in commuting and are the most difficult travel market for transit to serve.[1] To satisfy their suburban constituen-

cies, regional transit agencies in mature transit markets are often pressed to add or extend routes into suburban areas that are expensive to serve because the revenue potential is usually so much less than for the urban routes. Cash-starved agencies must often finance these improvements by cutting back service to current riders. This philosophy of "robbing Peter to pay Paul" can cost riders in the core constituency, the most profitable market segment, and run up expenses for the suburban service. Eventually, such a policy could require fare increases, which further reduce ridership and lead to a death spiral of cutbacks or more fare increases.

Building the market in the core constituency creates more of a win-win situation for the community. New housing in areas close to the downtown that are well served by transit will generate new transit riders and revenues with virtually no increase in service. With sufficient growth in riders, new service

is added, making transit even more convenient and attracting more riders.

One of the prime examples is New York City. After a decade of decline between 1980 and 1990, the population of Manhattan grew by 4 percent. The number of workers calling Manhattan home increased by 11 percent, and, complemented by improvements to bus and rail systems, commuting by transit increased by 145,000 for the decade. This was the largest transit gain of any metropolitan area and more than double the gain for the Washington, D.C., region, which was opening many new routes on its still-new subway.

A more typical, if extreme, example is St. Louis, which lost 12 percent of its residents between 1980 and 1990. Similar losses in the inner suburbs countered gains elsewhere, to limit the region to a mere 3 percent increase in regional population. Decentralization of jobs and other factors resulted in a huge 41 percent decline in com-

trict, in cooperation with the Hill Community Development Corporation, the Hill Project Area Committee, the Urban Redevelopment Authority, and the state and federal governments. The first phase consists of 203 rental apartments and townhouses and 27 for-sale houses; subsequent phases will offer more houses for sale. The completed project will include a swimming pool, sundeck, playground, and fitness center.

- In St. Paul, Robert Engstrom Companies developed Summit Place, a winner of the 1992 ULI Awards for Excellence that provides rental and ownership housing through a combination of

new construction and historic rehabilitation on an urban infill site in a deteriorated area.
- In Dallas, a new upscale community—the State-Thomas neighborhood—was created on 135 acres of mostly undeveloped land and freeway frontage near existing Victorian houses close to downtown Dallas. As a result of grass-roots advocacy by area residents and property owners, the State-Thomas planned development district was designated. This action provided a flexible planning framework and made possible city investments in the area funded through tax increment financing. For-profit developers initiated the new housing

muting by transit and a 42 percent loss in annual transit ridership between 1980 and 1990. Since the positive response to St. Louis's new MetroLink light-rail system in 1993, the region has been encouraging development opportunities around the stations in St. Louis, East St. Louis, and other inner-city locations.

Another transit success story in an unlikely setting is Houston. During the boom years of the early 1980s, transit plans developed a new light-rail system. Second thoughts and the subsequent economic downturn scrapped the plan in favor of a retooled bus system. Healthy growth in the city's population, combined with major bus improvements, helped double regional transit ridership.

The financial benefits of building transit ridership through building up rather than building out are clearly shown in the cost of new rail lines. It is estimated that in the United States, a typical city spent about $25,000 for each weekday rider on its new light-rail system, and normally

half of these passengers are former bus riders. Portland's regional transit operator, Tri-Met, is developing one of the most respected new light-rail systems and is emphasizing infill developments near the stations. A staff analysis of a joint development that generated 70 new riders estimated that developing ridership in this manner was eight to 20 times more effective than it would have been through rail extensions, *even if the land had been given to the developer* (the land cost the developer $130,000).

In addition to supporting transit, infill development can help reduce driving and regional congestion. For example, a project built in San Diego on the site of a former Sears store helped fill in an existing neighborhood with a food store, higher-density residential development, shops, and services. [2] Paul Buss, executive vice president of Oliver McMillan, the development partnership, said, "We were all surprised that 20 percent of the grocery store's business was pedestrian, which

is pretty unusual for southern California." Pedestrian activity seems to be significant for the new condominiums as well. Traffic counts showed that these units generate only four vehicle trips per day, compared with the six-trip average that engineers estimate is more typical of a project of that density (50 units per acre). It will be important, however, to acknowledge that such households are much more likely to have cars than to depend on walking, transit, and taxis. Adequate provision for parking and additional traffic must be made, but in most cases, making these improvements will be far less expensive than making improvements to accommodate suburban growth.

1. Alan E. Pisarski, *Commuting in America II* (Lansdowne, Va.: Eno Transportation Foundation, 1996), p. 73.
2. Robert T. Dunphy et al., *Moving Beyond Gridlock: Traffic and Development* (Washington, D.C.: Urban Land Institute, 1997), p. 136.

*Source:* Robert T. Dunphy, senior research director, ULI.

projects that became the State-Thomas neighborhood.
- In Milwaukee, Campus Circle, a multiple-use development by a subsidiary of Marquette University, includes 152 units of new student apartments above retail stores, plus 350 renovated units in nearby apartment buildings.
- In San Francisco, a nonprofit sponsor working with a for-profit turnkey developer created a 36-unit affordable housing project through the preservation, rehabilitation, and adaptive use of four auxiliary buildings of the historic Southern Pacific/Harkness Hospital complex in an ethnically diverse, mixed-income neighborhood.

- In New York City, Sparrow Construction, under the sponsorship of North General Hospital, recently completed in East Harlem the Maple Court Cooperative, a 135-unit elevator building surrounding a landscaped courtyard. The co-op's sharehold prices and maintenance charges are affordable to moderate-income families, who have been selected so far by lottery because the number of applicants has outnumbered the units available. A similar second phase is planned for construction later in 1997.

# Society Hill, Newark, New Jersey

Society Hill, the first low-rise housing development built in Newark in over 20 years, transformed a blighted area into an attractive and affordable community.

Society Hill demonstrates that low-rise, for-sale housing can be successfully developed in central cities if it is attractive, safe, and affordable.

The project is a 45-acre residential development located in a formerly blighted section of Newark, New Jersey. It features a variety of affordable, two- and three-bedroom condominiums and townhomes ranging in price from $93,000 to $130,000 and in size from 1,100 to 1,650 square feet.

The project is being built in five phases. As of 1993, Phases I and II (312 units) had been completed, and Phase III was underway, for a total of 600 homes.

The developer, K. Hovnanian Companies of Red Bank, New Jersey, created an attractive and affordable neighborhood where few residential developers will venture—downtown Newark. In fact, Society Hill is the first low-rise housing development to be built in Newark in over 20 years. It has also been one of the most successful. The first phase of homes (164 units) sold out in one weekend, and during the opening weekend for Phase II, more than 100 homes were sold.

Fifteen percent of the homes were reserved for low-income buyers, who received a generous discount on the price of a home. For example, a two-bedroom, two-story, 1,000-square-foot home at Society Hill, with a market price of about $100,000, sold for $28,000 to qualified low-income buyers. State grants helped to make up

the difference between the market and sales prices of such homes. With houses priced considerably below comparable homes in the Newark suburbs, Society Hill attracted buyers both from the Newark metropolitan area and from New York City.

## The Site

Society Hill occupies a site that was at the heart of the 1967 riots, which left a legacy of burned-out and largely abandoned buildings in Newark.

The bulk of the site was vacant property owned by the city. Before this land was redeveloped, fewer than 100 buildings remained on the site. All were demolished.

The project, which overlooks downtown Newark, stands between a community college and the University of Medicine and Dentistry of New Jersey. The site lies less than one mile from downtown Newark and Pennsylvania Station, and commuters can reach New York City from it by train or subway in about 20 minutes.

## Development and Financing

In 1985, a development company called Vogue Housing constructed 40 fee-simple townhouses called University Estates one block north of where Society Hill now stands. Before the project was completed, Hovnanian had formed a partnership with Vogue to build the first phase (164 units) of townhouses and condominiums at Society Hill. The partnership allowed Hovnanian, until then strictly a developer of townhomes and condominiums in the suburbs, to test the market in Newark.

Hovnanian then received approval to construct a mixed-use development consisting of about 100,000 square feet of commercial space and some 1,100 residential units on the 45-acre site. After the entire site had been declared a redevelopment area to make use of the city's eminent domain powers, the city acquired all of the properties and assisted in the relocation of families and businesses.

Both public and private monies were used to develop Society Hill. The entire project lies within a state urban enterprise zone created to spur economic development by offering financial incentives, such as lower taxes, to developers and employers that build within the zone. For example, the construction materials for Society Hill could be purchased tax-free. In addition, the Newark Economic Development Corporation (NEDC) received a $3.9 million Urban Development Action Grant from the state to help finance the proposed commercial center at Society Hill. The money will be used to help purchase the site and to prepare it for development, including the removal of contaminated soils. Hovnanian retains an option to purchase the site from the city for commercial development. NEDC envisions an $18 million, 100,000-square-foot shopping center with an anchor tenant occupying half of the center and the other half split among smaller stores.

## Design and Construction

Before buying the site, Hovnanian tested the entire property for chemical contamination, uncovering more than 7,000 cubic yards of contaminated soil, which were trucked to an approved hazardous waste landfill in Ohio. Soil with minor contamination was shipped to nearby landfills and used as cover.

In redesigning the site, which contained an existing grid of streets, the developer closed several streets to make parcels large enough so that townhouses could be grouped around parking courts. This design also allowed several parcels of open space to be scattered around the site. This plan has been phased in, and only the two smaller central parcels are complete. Later phases call for a retail center at the southwestern corner of the site and for recreational facilities (tennis courts and a swimming pool) on the northern portion.

The townhouses themselves are primarily two-level units stacked on top of two-level units. Each unit has its own ground-level entrance. Society Hill's Colonial architecture, open spaces, and spacious home designs were intended to mimic Hovnanian communities in the suburbs. The homes have vinyl or brick siding, central air conditioning, and electronic security systems. Many of the units feature garages and fireplaces.

## Experience Gained

- A large-scale residential development project in an urban area takes much longer, initially, to develop than it would take in the suburbs. When the project started, Newark's planning and approval process was not equipped to handle large residential projects efficiently.
- Estimates of site development costs for projects in urban areas must anticipate the possibility of having to clean up and stabilize contaminated soils.
- Through creative public/private partnerships, projects can be developed successfully in neglected urban areas.

*Source: ULI Project Reference File* report, Volume 23, Number 20.

# Summit Place, St. Paul, Minnesota

The 32 new and 12 restored apartments of Summit Place, with Summit Gardens Park in the foreground and St. Paul's Cathedral in the background.

Summit Place is a pioneering urban infill development that combines new construction with the rehabilitation of existing structures. The project, which won a ULI Award for Excellence, contains a mix of single-family detached houses, townhouses, condominiums, and rental apartments. With 97 units on 5.5 acres, it has a gross density of 17.8 units per acre, and more than half of the land area is open space.

Construction on Summit Place began in 1977 and was completed in 1986. Development of the project has recreated a positive neighborhood image and has provided the impetus for economic and physical revitalization in the surrounding community. Today, 20 years after project construction began, commercial activity is occurring once again on adjacent Selby Avenue, once considered blighted.

## Planning

The project stands within a mile of downtown St. Paul on a two-and-a-half-block site on Cathedral Hill in St. Paul's historic Ramsey Hill neighborhood, an older residential area that contains many large historic structures dating from the late 1800s. When the Summit Place project was initiated, much of the neighborhood had deteriorated. Buildings had been abandoned, and occupied buildings had been subdivided into small rooming units. In addition, Selby Avenue adjacent to the site

had an extremely poor image among residents of the Twin Cities. Another adjacent street, Summit Avenue, however, was well regarded.

The developer, Robert Engstrom, worked closely with the Ramsey Hill Association from the outset of the project, responding to its concerns and convincing it that the development would preserve the character, scale, and fabric of the existing neighborhood. As a result, the neighborhood association supported Engstrom at city hearings. The city responded by giving flexible development agreements, allowing building setback and height variances, vacating several existing alleys that crossed the site, and approving rear-access garages.

A combination of public and private funds financed the $9 million project. The city of St. Paul provided below-market-rate permanent financing ($3.8 million) through the sale of revenue bonds. In addition, it made available HUD Section 312 funds

and credit-enhanced financing for rental housing. A local bank offered construction financing through a revolving loan.

## Design

Summit Place preserved the neighborhood fabric in ways similar to those advocated today by the promoters of traditional neighborhood development (TND), or "the new urbanism." It was designed to retain the character and historic nature of the neighborhood by carefully blending the restoration of existing buildings with new construction. Existing buildings that were restored include single-family, detached houses; duplexes; condominiums (including a carriage house that was converted to four condominium units); and a 12-unit, three-story rental apartment building.

Exteriors of the existing structures were meticulously restored to retain their architectural character. For example, three of the existing single-family detached houses—referred to as the "sister houses" because of their similar designs—had been covered with Depression siding or asphalt, imitation-brick shingles. These coverings were removed; the original wood siding was cleaned and painted; damaged or missing Victorian details were restored; and the houses were reroofed, given new chimneys, and fitted with wooden combination windows. Exteriors of other buildings were sandblasted to remove old paint and then repainted. Interiors of most of the existing buildings are contemporary in design, and units feature energy-saving insulation, skylights, exposed brick walls, fireplaces, high ceilings, balconies, custom-built kitchen cabinets, and upgraded appliances.

The new buildings—primarily townhouses and rental apartments—were designed to reflect Victorian elements and to fit with the scale and character of the existing buildings and the surrounding neighborhood. For example, the first of the new buildings to be constructed, a three-unit townhouse, uses contemporary exterior materials (redwood siding stained a bluish gray), but its size and its steeply pitched rooflines are compatible with the large single-family houses in the area. The careful integration of older, restored historic structures and new construction was designed to produce a distinct neighborhood identity.

Buildings back up on landscaped, common open space in the center of each block, and a small park on the corner of one block provides additional open space. Vacated alleyways connect open areas and discourage through-traffic by pedestrians and automobiles. Both interior and street-side open space is attractively landscaped. "Found materials," such as alley pavers, contribute to an interesting streetscape.

Summit Place was targeted at the middle-income market, and many units were presold. Buyers were primarily young professional couples, although they ranged from young singles to empty nesters. The 54 rental units in three buildings are owned and managed by the developer, who also owns and maintains the intensively landscaped urban park.

In 1996, the city of St. Paul cooperated with Robert and Phyllis Engstrom, the homeowners' association, and the adjacent homeowners in restoring Maiden Lane with the original brick pavers. This is now a common route for pedestrians and for the historic tours that originate at the nearby James J. Hill Mansion.

## Experience Gained

- An infill project in a rundown area should be large enough to create its own environment. The availability of a contiguous two-and-a-half-block site under single ownership made sufficient size possible at Summit Place. Furthermore, initial development should be concentrated in one location, not scattered over various lots. This will produce a sample of the total environment later on, thereby maximizing the impact and marketability of the project as soon as possible.
- The cooperation of the city and the support of local neighborhood residents were important to the project's success. The city's approval of the developer's request for variances provided the flexibility needed so that new construction could be sensitively integrated with existing structures. The city also assigned a staff member as the "project manager" for Summit Place, which enabled the developer and the city to resolve their problems expeditiously.
- Locating open space in the center of the block proved to be a wise step. Because it offers a sense of security, residents use this space frequently. The open space also affords pleasant views from many units.
- Summit Place embodies many of the principles of traditional neighborhood development, such as sidewalks, short setbacks, rear-loaded garages, and a pleasant street appearance. An important variable is the irregularly shaped blocks, which have permitted landscaped open space in the centers of the blocks. Twenty years after the start of development, Robert Engstrom comments that it is much easier to accomplish traditional neighborhood development on an infill site rather than in a new development in the suburbs.

*Source: ULI Project Reference File* report, Volume 15, Number 1.

# Pine Street Cottages, Seattle, Washington

The public sides of the rehabilitated bungalows of Pine Street Cottages in Seattle, Washington, were kept mostly intact; front porches were enclosed to create small front halls.

Pine Street Cottages is a tenunit, cottage renovation development that has provided affordable for-sale, single-family houses in a transitional inner-city neighborhood close to downtown Seattle. Targeted at working professionals, the cottages were sold as individual condominiums to first-time buyers, who were otherwise priced out of in-city home-ownership.

The project is located on a relatively flat one-third-acre site within a predominantly single-family traditional neighborhood. The previously blighted area is increasingly attractive to buyers in search of close-in, low-cost housing. Built in 1916, the Craftsman-style cottages had been abandoned for a decade

and were prime candidates for demolition.

When John Kucher and his partner, George Rutherford, first purchased the cottages and two adjacent single-family houses, they envisioned a far less ambitious renovation consisting mainly of external cosmetic changes. The decision to undertake a major renovation with high-quality finishes was prompted by the realization that this was a one-time opportunity to set a precedent for this type of multifamily product (proscribed under current zoning) within a traditional single-family neighborhood.

The sides of the cottages that faced the streets were generally kept intact. Most of the design changes were made to the backs

facing an inner community courtyard and to the unit interiors. Interiors were gutted to make the 400-square-foot-plus units function more efficiently and feel more spacious.

## Planning and Design

As part of the space-stretching program, the original ceilings and attics were replaced with vaulted ceilings and open beams. A loft over the bedroom closet and kitchen that adds 100 square feet to each cottage also creates additional storage/sleeping space. The ten-foot-by-ten-foot loft space was set up to function as a bedroom and is fully equipped with carpeting, an operable skylight, telephone jack, light switch, and electrical outlet. An adjacent ceiling fan helps circulate air to the loft.

The kitchen and bedroom were flipped so that the bedroom and bathroom could be sealed off from the more public living room and kitchen spaces, behind a pocket door. The living room is large enough for a sofa and several chairs. Large skylights, three of which can be opened, provide natural light and ventilation. The kitchen is compact but efficiently organized: three people can fit around the L-shaped counter.

Each cottage was given a new roof and hardwood floors. Where feasible, elements from the original interiors were saved, such as the old multipaned windows. New items replicated the old style: shingle siding, old-fashioned faucets, and brass address numerals.

Some alterations were aimed at strengthening safety. For example, each front door, facing the street, was relocated at a right angle by enclosing part of the original exterior porch. The front door then became more visible from the street, helping to discourage break-ins. Enclosure of the porch also created a small front hall, with space enough for a hat and coat rack, and a more gracious entryway. An alarm system was installed that consisted of contact sensors on doors, a motion detector, and a panic button. For an additional fee, the system can be linked with a central monitoring station that notifies the police when the alarm is triggered. On the outside, automatic locking gates secure the courtyard and parking areas.

The interior courtyard—the primary community space—is a lush garden with a central lawn and brick seating area. The perimeter plantings are mainly of culinary herbs and small fruit trees that homeowners are free to pick. Garden maintenance is included in the $90-a-month condominium fee. Pedestrian paths strategically cut through the courtyard in ways to encourage neighborly interaction. Paths lead from the secured parking area through the courtyard to the cottages' backyards and to the mailboxes behind the entry gate. Next to the mailboxes is a bench on which residents can rest their bags of groceries while removing their mail from mailboxes.

The architect intended each cottage's deck to supplement the shared open spaces. The decks have white wooden trellises with an identifying vine for every cottage: clematis, rose, or wisteria. The decks have built-in benches, a feature that discourages outdoor furniture clutter.

Lanterns disguised as green metal tulips provide soft downlighting in the courtyard. Set on automatic timers, the lights help secure the parking lot and courtyard at night.

## Approvals and Financing

The developer estimates that between $8,000 and $12,000 a unit would have been saved had the cottages been built from scratch. The cramped one-half-foot crawl space significantly drove up construction costs. Under the current single-family zoning for the site, however, construction would have been limited to two larger—and, most likely, more expensive— detached houses.

When the developer started applying for construction loans in June 1990, the S&L debacle was prompting a host of new financing constraints, like new appraisal requirements, which delayed financing for the project by several months. Construction loan financing was finally obtained from Seafirst Bank. Because the cottages were located within a CRA area, as designated under the Community Reinvestment Act, Seafirst was interested in financing the project as a way to garner CRA bonus points, which would help further its social responsibility goals and aid in future bank transactions.

Significant alterations to the cottage interiors and exteriors disqualified the cottages from designation as Seattle historic landmarks. Renovation of the interior courtyard and the system of interconnecting walkways, however, were sufficiently close to the original plan to warrant preservation status. Under the city's preservation laws, owners of historically preserved properties are permitted to deduct certain renovation expenses from assessed property valuations for ten years. For example, the purchaser of a cottage that sold for $86,000 is taxed as if the property were valued at $26,000, which translates into a savings of about $700 per year for ten years.

One of the requirements for qualifying for FHA loans is that apartments that have been converted to condominiums must have had condominium declarations and surveys in place for at least a year before HUD will consider guaranteeing the project. HUD agreed to waive the one-year requirement and to treat the development as new construction so that the cottages could qualify for FHA financing. As a result, purchasers only had to pay about $7,000 as a downpayment, including closing costs.

## Experience Gained

- The developer wanted to achieve a culturally and racially mixed buyer profile. But the initial marketing program, which entailed mailing brochures describing the project to different multiethnic organizations and churches, was not effective in achieving this goal. Instead of relying on passive printed materials, the developer learned that he needed to go to the churches and community centers and to meet directly with potential purchasers.

- As much specificity as possible is recommended in drafting condominium declarations. Given the tight space constraints of this project, it was important to limit the number of persons to occupy each cottage. Children were

permitted, but no more than two persons were allowed to live in each unit. Likewise, rules regarding pets should be stated explicitly. Because purchasers are frequently put off by voluminous condominium agreements, the developer is considering producing a video that would highlight the important elements of the agreement for future projects.

- This project demonstrates a strong demand for affordable, modest-sized detached

units close to downtown. People are willing to trade square footage for homeownership, detached units, high-quality finishes, and amenities such as landscaped courtyards, off-street parking, and wooden decks.

*Source: ULI Project Reference File* report, Volume 22, Number 16.

## Chapter Notes

1. Eli Ginsberg, "The Changing Urban Scene: 1960–90 and Beyond," in Henry Cisneros, editor, *Interwoven Destinies*, Eighty-Second American Assembly, Columbia University, April 15–18, 1993 (participants' edition), pp. 6–7 of the article.

2. William H. Frey and Elaine L. Fielding, "Changing Urban Populations: Regional Restructuring, Racial Polarization, and Poverty Concentration," in *Cityscape*, Volume 1, Number 2 (Washington, D.C.: U.S. Department of Housing and Urban Development, Office of Policy Development and Research, June 1995), p. 14.

3. Franklin J. James, "Urban Economics: Trends, Forces, and Implications for the President's National Urban Policy," *Cityscape*, Volume 1, Number 2 (Washington, D.C.: U.S. Department of Housing and Urban Development, Office of Policy Development and Research, June 1995), p. 67.

4. Anthony Downs, *New Visions for Metropolitan America* (Washington, D.C.: Brookings Institution; and Cambridge, Mass.: Lincoln Institute of Land Policy; 1994), p. 53.

5. Keith R. Ihlanfeldt, "The Importance of the Central City to the Regional and National Economy: A Review of the Empirical Evidence," *Cityscape*, Volume 1, Number 2 (June 1995), p. 126.

6. Ihlanfeldt, "The Importance of the Central City to the Regional and National Economy," p. 127.

7. Downs, *New Visions for Metropolitan America*, p. 53.

8. Elliot Sclar and Walter Hook, "The Importance of Cities to the National Economy," in Henry Cisneros, editor, *Interwoven Destinies*, p. 3 of the article.

9. Sclar and Hook, "The Importance of Cities to the National Economy," p. 2.

10. James, "Urban Economics," p. 67.

11. For example, according to Larry C. Ledebur and William R. Barnes, *All in It Together: Cities, Suburbs, and Economic Regions* (Washington, D.C.: National League of Cities, February 1993), an analysis of 78 metropolitan areas showed that changes in city and suburban incomes over a ten-year period tended to be directly related.

12. Downs, *New Visions for Metropolitan America*, p. 52.

13. See Richard W. Huffman, "A New Look at Inner-City Housing," *Urban Land*, Volume 56, Number 1 (January 1997); Lew Sichelman, "Converting Offices to Homes," *Urban Land*, Volume 56, Number 1 (January 1997); and Diane R. Suchman, "Transforming Public Housing Developments into Mixed-Income Comunities," ULI Working Paper 653 (June 1996).

14. Nancy Bragado, Judy Corbett, and Sharon Sprowls, *Building Livable Communities: A Policymaker's Guide to Infill Development* (Washington, D.C.: Center for Livable Communities and Local Government Commission, 1995), p. 3.

15. Local Housing Element Assistance Project, *Blueprint for Bay Area Housing* (San Francisco: Bay Area Council and Association of Bay Area Governments, no publication date given), p. 57.

## CHAPTER 2

# Assessing the Market for Infill Housing

*Information for this chapter was provided by Margaret Sowell of Neighborhood Strategies, Inc., Wayne, Pennsylvania.*

The process of developing housing on infill sites is fundamentally similar to that for any residential development. As with any kind of development, the developer needs to consider the level and nature of likely market demand and of the existing and potential competition, and to assess how easily and under what terms the land can be acquired. The history and physical characteristics of the land—its topography, subsoil (e.g., remnants of previous uses), drainage, access, and the presence of any environmental contaminants—as well as an understanding of neighborhood dynamics and all applicable governmental requirements and development approvals, are important ingredients in the feasibility analysis. Moreover, the developer must consider the project's likely costs in light of the potential income the project can realistically generate before working with public agencies and private lenders to obtain financing.

Many for-profit developers shy away from inner-city housing development because of these issues and because they do not perceive a market there. In fact, markets often do exist and may be even stronger than in outlying areas. Or a market can be created. This chapter outlines the process of assessing inner-city housing markets.

## Factors Determining Demand

The primary motive for developing infill sites is to capture expanding markets. Often, the market for infill housing is generated by the strengthening service economy and by growth in centrally located office employment. Also to be considered are the large proportion of single or childless households and the "pool" of existing or former city residents, people who must live in the city because they have jobs there, and people who are interested in access to urban amenities.

Inner-city neighborhoods have certain advantages: infill locations are often accessible to public transit and close to employment centers—particularly "anchor institutions" like hospitals or universities—and to commercial services, and parks. They are found in established neighborhoods that are often distinct architecturally, have mature landscaping, and represent cultural or historic resources.

Existing residents have a stake in the neighborhood, and many would like to stay. Some residents of other city neighborhoods would be attracted to better housing in an infill location if it were available. Many former residents who live elsewhere retain ties to the neighborhood through, for example, relatives or church affiliations, and some would be interested in returning if attractive housing were to be found.

The diverse pool of downtown workers—especially service sector workers employed by large downtown institutions—who would prefer to live near their work are clearly one category of demand for infill housing developments. Other categories include committed urbanites and "urban pioneers," current city residents seeking homeownership opportunities, and former city residents who would return to their old neighborhoods if better housing were located there. Because schools are

# What Is a Market Analysis?

**A** market analysis is an assessment of the level and nature of demand for a particular type of real estate project, and it should be performed by a professional real estate market analyst. In most cases, its purpose is to provide information on how a property—either an existing development or a proposed new project—will perform. For residential projects, for example, the market analysis usually provides information on the demand for a specified number of housing units at a specific location, the likely rental or sales prices that housing units will command if they are placed on the market at an identified time, and the estimated absorption rate or sales pace, i.e., an estimate of the average number of houses that will be rented or sold each month. Sometimes, a market analysis also will include a cash flow projection showing the estimated revenues and expenses of the real estate project as a basis for determining whether the operation of the property will generate sufficient income to yield an acceptable return on the capital that will be invested to purchase or develop it.

Although there are variations, a typical market analysis for a residential development involves the following:

- *An analysis of the site or location of the proposed project.* Analyses will typically determine whether surrounding land uses are compatible with housing development and whether community facilities and services are available to support residential development.

- *An economic analysis of national, regional, and local conditions that will affect the project's performance.* Economic factors such as employment, income characteristics, migration/business location considerations, and the presence or absence of growth controls usually are considered, as they may affect the demand for housing of the type proposed.

- *An assessment of demand.* Factors considered include population and household growth, together with analyses of the age distribution of households and household income. Demand is generally evaluated within primary and secondary housing market areas that are drawn specifically for the project. A housing market area is defined as the geographic boundaries within which households will choose a residential unit from available choices.

- *An analysis of supply, that is, of the real estate products that would compete with the proposed project in the market area.* This analysis considers the availability, price, size, location, and characteristics of existing units, as well as of planned and proposed developments, that will compete with the proposed projects for buyers or renters within the identified market area. For rental units, the analysis will include occupancy levels and numbers of vacant units by size. For for-sale units, this analysis will cover the absorption

an issue for families with children and because many central cities have troubled school systems, the most likely potential market segments are single people; young, empty-nester, or gay couples without children; and elderly people.

Local market dynamics driving residential demand differ from city to city. The potential for infill housing is greater in metropolitan areas where the demand for housing is generally strong and prices for housing are high, relative to incomes. This is especially true if suburban growth is restricted by regulation or geography (although such conditions will also likely result in high land costs). As a rule, in metropolitan areas where housing demand is soft, where home prices are generally affordable, and where suburban growth is unrestricted, infill development is riskier, though probably less expensive than elsewhere.

Pinpointing the target market within a specific neighborhood is more problematic, especially in parts of the city where no new development has occurred for many years and where there are no comparable projects to evaluate.

The remainder of this chapter gives guidance on how to evaluate the potential market for a specific project proposal in an inner-city neighborhood.

rate by type of unit, the total number of units already sold, and the number of units yet to be sold, including homes planned for future phases of the development.

- *An assessment of the project's likely performance, based on an estimate of the portion of the market that the property will capture.* Capture rates are "educated," professional judgments based on as much factual information as can be assembled. Nonetheless, the performance of a property in future years always will be affected by some circumstances and conditions that cannot be anticipated or predicted.

- *Recommendations of ways to enhance the project's market demand, rental rates or sales prices, and absorption rate.*

Market analyses are used primarily by developers, property owners, lenders, local governments, and others to determine a proposed project's value, how that potential value can be enhanced, and whether and how much money, time, and/

or effort should be invested in the project.

Although this point may seem obvious, it is critical that there be a mutual understanding between the developer/sponsor and the market analyst about the purpose of the market analysis, the specific questions that are to be addressed and answered, and the type of development that is proposed. For example, if the inner-city housing that is proposed involves rehabilitation or adaptive use of an existing structure or preservation of a historic building, there may be constraints inherent in the size or configuration of the structure(s) that will affect the project's ability to respond to market conditions. Similarly, the market analyst needs to know if a percentage of the units will be income-restricted, so that he or she can measure demand on that basis.

The market analyst also should understand the intended use of the housing market analysis. If the analysis is to be submitted to a lender, some

consulting firms will want assurances or indemnifications to protect against future liability, or there may be special procedures to be followed to permit this type of use. In addition, lenders may have specific requirements relating to their approval processes, or they may want information to be supplied as it must appear on loan application forms. State housing finance agencies may require the market analyst to complete the agencies' prescribed forms. If financing is related to the types of households that will occupy the housing units, like first-time homebuyers, this factor will affect calculations of demand. Thus, a clear understanding of the market analysis assignment can help ensure that the resulting product will yield information appropriate to the intended purpose.

*Source:* Neighborhood Strategies, Inc., Wayne, Pennsylvania.

## Issues in Inner-City Housing Markets

Market analyses for housing developments proposed in inner-city neighborhoods must consider a number of special issues and concerns that will affect the projects' performance. Many inner-city neighborhoods are challenging development environments because of physical conditions such as deteriorated infrastructure, patterns of disinvestment and abandonment, and a lack of supporting facilities and services like grocery stores and convenience retail outlets. Inner-city areas often are losing population and households, and

there may be high vacancy rates in existing housing. Hence, a traditional demand analysis will suggest that there are few or no new households to occupy additional units that might be provided, and statistics may show that on a gross basis there is an ample supply of housing to meet the needs of current residents.

Issues of economic conditions, household income, community participation, environmental conditions, and state and local housing requirements deter many developers more accustomed to suburban "greenfield" sites and to expanding the numbers of potential occupants of new and rehabilitated units.

Yet there often is very strong demand for inner-city housing that has been developed to meet the needs of present and potential residents. When such circumstances exist, developers and sponsors are rewarded for their efforts both financially and emotionally, by having created a new residential environment for residents and contributed to community revitalization.

Fortunately, much more information exists today than could be tapped in past years, and local officials responsible for inner-city neighborhoods will often assist the members of a development team in identifying sources of data and useful studies. In addition, as discussed in Chapter 6, local officials may be willing to help in other ways, for example, by providing improvements to inner-city neighborhoods that make for a more supportive environment for the proposed housing development. And, as outlined in Chapter 5, they may assist developers and sponsors in tapping federal, state, and local funding sources to help finance the development.

## Evaluating the Project Location and Surroundings

Demand will be influenced by the general characteristics of the location, the site itself, and the surrounding neighborhood. (Site selection information is described in Chapter 3, which covers development considerations.) The site and any structures that will be reused must be physically suitable for the intended development, and the costs associated with preparing the site and rehabilitating the structures must be factored into the project's market and feasibility analyses.

The character of the surrounding neighborhood and community will also affect the project's marketability and must be factored into the analysis. Community response to the proposed project, whether positive or negative, is also important. To some extent, a wise developer can work with the city and the community to improve the physical, social, and economic conditions in the nearby area and enhance the project's market potential and long-term sustainability.

## Performing an Economic Analysis

An economic analysis will ascertain how economic conditions and trends in the United States, the region, and the city overall will affect demand for a specific inner-city housing development. Key indicators include employment patterns and growth, such as whether or not the regional economy is prospering, which sectors of the economy are growing, and which sectors are declining. Related issues are whether or not the regional or local economy is dependent on a single industry or industrial sector and whether that sector is stable, growing, or declining.

The following questions are relevant to understanding the economic environment within which a particular inner-city housing development is proposed:

- Is the economy growing and generating new employees who will require housing?
- Is unemployment projected to be stable or to decline, boosting consumers' confidence in their ability to purchase or rent housing when the housing units are being marketed?
- Are the population and number of households in the region increasing, fueling demand for additional housing units; or, as in many large northeastern and midwestern cities, is the rate of population and household decline slowing?
- Are household incomes increasing, so that additional families will be able to afford the housing that is proposed?
- Does the city have a favorable economic outlook, based on its ability to attract new businesses?
- What age patterns does the population exhibit, and what inferences can be drawn about the types of housing that will be required to meet emerging needs?

## Assessing Housing Demand

Demand for a proposed inner-city housing development will be determined by the demographic characteristics of the households present in the market area, whether the population is growing and/or changing, and whether the households now residing or expected to reside in the market area will need more housing units or will desire new or different kinds of residential units. Demand for housing is generated by growth in the numbers of households or changes in the composition of households already residing in the area, by the need to replace housing units that are physically or functionally obsolete, and by assumptions about households not now living in the area who could reasonably be expected to want to live there.

# Figure I. Ellen Wilson Demographics

This table, prepared for a market analysis of an inner-city housing project on Capitol Hill in Washington, D.C., is an example of summary demographic information related to housing demand. As the data show, declines in population and in numbers of households were major concerns in ascertaining whether demand existed for the housing units proposed.

## Selected Economic and Demographic Characteristics

| | District of Columbia | Capitol Hill Market Area | Ellen Wilson Tracts |
|---|---|---|---|
| **Population** | | | |
| 1980 Census | 638,333 | 41,866 | 8,334 |
| 1990 Census | 606,900 | 38,583 | 6,635 |
| Percent Change 1980–1990 | –4.9% | –7.8% | -20.4% |
| Average Annual Percent Change, 1980–1990 | –0.5% | –0.8% | –2.3% |
| 1995 Estimate | 563,732 | 36,048 | 5,943 |
| Percent Change, 1990–1995 | –7.1% | –6.6% | –10.4% |
| Average Annual Percent Change, 1990–1995 | –2.8% | –1.4% | –2.2% |
| 2000 Projection | 526,044 | 33,740 | 5,391 |
| Percent Change, 1995–2000 | –6.7% | –6.4% | –9.3% |
| Average Annual Percent Change, 1995–2000 | –1.4% | –1.3% | –1.9% |
| **Households** | | | |
| 1980 Census | 253,144 | 17,229 | 3,620 |
| 1990 Census | 249,634 | 17,103 | 3,038 |
| Percent Change, 1980–1990 | –1.4% | –0.7% | –16.1% |
| 1995 Estimate | 235,568 | 16,237 | 2,745 |
| Percent Change, 1990–1995 | –5.6% | –5.1% | –9.6% |
| Average Annual Percent Change, 1990–1995 | 1.2% | –1.0% | –2.0% |
| 2000 Projection | 223,768 | 15,479 | 2,510 |
| Percent Change, 1995–2000 | –5.0% | –4.7% | 0.9% |
| Average Annual Percent Change, 1995–2000 | –1.0% | –1.0% | –1.8% |
| **Median Household Income** | | | |
| 1989 Figures from 1990 Census | $30,725 | $39,927 | $36,034 |
| 1995 Estimate | $37,449 | $51,916 | $45,525 |
| Percent Change, 1989–1995 | 21.9% | 30.0% | 26.3% |
| Average Annual Percent Change, 1989–1995 | 3.4% | 4.5% | 4.0% |
| 2000 Projection | $42,637 | $59,728 | $53,022 |
| Percent Change, 1995–2000 | 13.9% | 15.0% | 16.5% |
| Average Annual Percent Change, 1995–2000 | 2.6% | 2.8% | 3.1% |
| **Average Household Size** | | | |
| 1990 Census | 2.26 | 2.17 | 1.91 |
| 1995 Estimate | 2.22 | 2.13 | 1.86 |
| 2000 Projection | 2.17 | 2.08 | 1.82 |
| **Median Age in 1995** (in years) | 34.9 | 35.7 | 34.4 |
| **1995 Population by Race** (percent) | | | |
| White (not Hispanic) | 28.6% | 45.1% | 61.3% |
| African American (not Hispanic) | 64.3% | 51.3% | 34.6% |
| Asian | 2.3% | 1.6% | 2.0% |
| Hispanic | 4.3% | 1.6% | 1.7% |
| All Other | 0.4% | 0.4% | 0.4% |
| **Housing Units** | | | |
| 1980 Census | 276,987 | 19,236 | 3,948 |
| 1990 Census | 278,489 | 19,284 | 3,797 |
| Percent Change, 1980–1990 | 0.5% | 0.3% | –3.8% |
| Average Annual Percent Change, 1980–1990 | 0.5% | 0.0% | –0.4% |
| 1995 Estimate | 269,855 | 18,861 | 3,605 |
| Percent Change, 1990–1995 | –3.1% | –2.2% | –5.1% |
| Average Annual Percent Change, 1990–1995 | –0.6% | –0.4% | –0.5% |
| 2000 Projection | 256,259 | 17,985 | 3,291 |
| Percent Change, 1995–2000 | –5.1% | –4.6% | –8.7% |
| Average Annual Percent Change, 1995–2000 | –1.0% | –0.9% | –1.8% |

*Sources:* U.S. Bureau of the Census; Claritas Corporation; and Real Estate Strategies, Inc.

A new senior citizens' residence, shown under construction at First Ward Place in Charlotte, North Carolina.

In assessing market demand, Fred Kober, president of The Christopher Companies in McLean, Virginia, cautions that the market research must include, as far as possible, ascertaining not only that a market will exist when a project opens but also that the market has enough depth to ensure sufficient demand through the life of the project.

In inner cities, it is quite likely that demographic data alone will paint a dismal picture of an area experiencing population and household declines and having concentrations of low-income households. Without additional analysis, it may be easy to conclude that no demand exists at all. But in-depth interviews with realtors, real estate sales personnel, property managers, and knowledgeable officials of any large employer or institution located in the market area can help identify other factors in the market area that will influence or generate demand for infill housing development in inner-city neighborhoods. Qualitative information can also be obtained from meetings or focus groups with identified potential residents.

Special conditions can also affect housing demand. For example, many large cities have a residency requirement for some or all municipal employees. These employees—most of whom are middle-income—can be sources of solid demand for an inner-city housing development, especially

for new homes in older communities where little new housing has been constructed.

Institutions in inner cities—most notably hospitals and educational institutions—have large numbers of employees, some of whom may be interested in living close to work. In college and university neighborhoods, students who must seek off-campus housing when dormitory rooms are not provided add to the demand for nearby apartments. Especially when an inner-city neighborhood is perceived as safe and is convenient, an inner-city housing development can usually tap a portion of the demand that an institution generates. For instance, the Cleveland Clinic, on the East Side of Cleveland, has provided a positive impetus for redevelopment of the nearby Hough area. Once initial revitalization activity had gained momentum, the Hough community began to attract municipal employees affected by city residency requirements.

In addition, many city neighborhoods contain large ethnic populations in well-established communities or in concentrations resulting from recent immigration. These ethnic communities may want or need more or different housing alternatives, and in some cities, they may constitute significant sources of potential demand. Some ethnic groups have cultural preferences in housing that are important to consider in project or unit design. Qualitative information to help the developer understand the needs and preferences of these potential markets can be obtained from interviews, community organizations, and focus-group research.

In sum, the purpose of the demand analysis is to use demographic data, along with information obtained in interviews, to determine whether it is reasonable to expect that there will be households that will want to live in the housing units being proposed. Because the housing proposed for inner-city neighborhoods may target a different mix of households from the one that currently resides in the area, or may seek to attract households as part of a concerted revitalization effort, it usually is not possible to identify demand for a proposed inner-city housing development based on demographic characteristics alone.

## Analyzing the Competitive Housing Supply

The performance of other housing available in the market area or areas, especially housing similar to the proposed development, provides an indication of the proposed project's potential for success. It can also suggest steps to take and actions to avoid in developing the concept for a new property.

Of course, information on the supply of housing in the market area should include overall trends in the market area, including numbers or percentages of owner-occupied and rental housing units; data on new permits issued and housing units recently constructed or rehabilitated; trends in sales prices, number of days on the market, and sales pace for sales houses; and, for rental apartments, vacancy rates, occupancy trends, and rents. This information is very helpful in understanding general supply conditions that will affect the proposed development. Then, however, information should be gathered on relevant housing developments in the market area, to help in determining which ones may be regarded as competitors. Detailed information should be obtained on each competitive project, including an evaluation of its competitive position relative to the proposed development and comments on its likely effects on the proposed project.

Households seeking residential units in a particular part of a city usually have a number of choices, so it is important to talk to realtors active in the market area to obtain information on the characteristics of the existing housing stock

and on recent sales or rental activity. This information should include absorption or vacancy rates in the target area, pricing, and buyer or renter profiles. Building permit data, usually available from local government agencies, can afford guidance on additions to the housing stock and on how development activity has changed over time. The number of housing demolitions and the number of substandard housing units, though this is difficult information to obtain, are two other important indicators of housing conditions and availability in the area.

Maxine Mitchell, president of Applied Real Estate Analysis in Chicago, agrees. According to Mitchell, the developer needs to talk to realtors to learn the profile of people who are looking for houses in the city, where they want to locate, where they actually move, and why they are making those choices. Her firm also talks with community leaders and surveys church congregations to obtain information on specific neighborhoods. Where no new housing has been built, the existing housing stock is the major competition; it gives clues on what people can get for their money and on what problems they are buying into, as well. Using this information, the developer can estimate the premium that buyers might be willing to pay for a new house.

Mitchell indicates that market issues are even more complicated in African American communities, where lack of housing choices and lack of access to financing have resulted in little turnover and therefore fewer resales to evaluate, and where houses have not appreciated as much as in other neighborhoods.

After all of the information on the existing housing supply has been completed and analyzed, and once the market trends and market conditions are understood, judgments must be made regarding which of the housing options available to consumers within the market area will be the proposed development's competitors. Factors to be considered include proximity to the proposed location, type of housing, price structure, similarity of the anticipated target market, and features and amenities offered. For example, a newly constructed for-sale development with similarly priced units located in the same neighborhood would be expected to compete directly for buyers with a proposed for-sale, infill development; a substantially rehabilitated historic factory offering upscale rental units would compete with another historic rehabilitation of a rental property in the same neighborhood.

# Figure 2. Wilmington Competitors

This analysis of competitive for-sale properties was compiled on the basis of interviews with developers and sales representatives that were conducted in connection with a Wilmington, Delaware, market analysis. As the table shows, the interview process was designed to elicit information on the units and their pricing, features, and sales pace. Although not shown on the table, buyer profiles also were requested during the interviews.

## Analysis of Competitive Projects

| Project Name and Address | Units Sold/ Number of Units | Under Contract | Square Feet in Units | Number of Bedrooms | Number of Baths | Purchase Price | Price/ Square Foot | Amenities/Extras |
|---|---|---|---|---|---|---|---|---|
| Christiana Court 14th & 15th at Claymont and Heald | 21 | 21 | 1,000– 1,100 | 3 | 1.5 | $66,000 | $60.00– $66.00 | Garages Project sold out in two years |
| Coyne Park 14th & Heald | 25 | 23 | 1,200 | 2 and 3 | 1.5 | $67,500– $69,500 | $55.75– $56.67 | Ten units with garages Some with appliances W/D hookups |
| Kings Grant 12th & Heald | 23 (52 planned) | 23 | 1,120 | 3 | 1.5 | $68,900 | $59.82 | Off-street parking W/D hookups All-brick construction |
| Elliott Run 21st & West | 33 | 11/3 | 1,600 | 3 | 1.5 | $91,900- $95,900 | $57.44– $59.94 | Off-street parking Security fencing Full basement Appliances |
| Curlett Place 7th & Church | 13 | 3/0 | 1,190 | 3 | 1.5 | $59,900 | $50.34 | Off-street parking Full basement |
| Riverview Terrace at Fox Point 30th & Heald | 24 | 0/0 | 1,265– 1,290 | 3 | 1.5 | $83,900 | $66.32– $65.04 | Off-street parking Full basement Kitchen appliances Free refrigerator for first ten purchasers |
| 34th & Tatnall (proposed) | 10 | 0/0 | 1,265– 1,290 | 3 | 1.5 | $83,900 | $66.32– $65.04 | Same as Riverview Terrace, except brick construction |

*Source:* Interviews conducted by Real Estate Strategies, Inc.

Unfortunately, such situations, in which there is another development that is obviously comparable in all respects and will compete head-on for the same occupants, rarely occur in inner-city neighborhoods. A competitive for-sale subdivision may be located outside the primary housing market area; a historic rehabilitation property may be a condominium instead of a rental property; or new construction may compete with a rehabilitation. Even two apparently direct competitors may have locations on different streets that make a difference; or one may be adjacent to the central business district, while the other is to be sited in a more remote portion of the same market area. Moreover, it is always important to remember that a property that is already built will have its own reputation in the market, whether positive or negative, and that this will affect its competitive position.

Information on a number of different, potentially competitive properties should be used to inform judgments on the proposed development and how it will perform. For example, a rental housing development for seniors may compete with a proposed development that will not be age-restricted but that expects to attract some older residents. A mixed-income development may compete for tenants who will pay market rents. A subsidized new-construction project may compete with a proposed unsubsidized development offering new units for sale.

Analysis of competitive projects should include the following information:

- Description of the housing, including number of units, styles and square footages of units, age, general physical condition, location, and surrounding neighborhood characteristics.
- Identity of the developer and of the management or marketing company or property manager.
- Amenities and features offered in the units and available on site.
- Sales or rental prices, including any special promotions or concessions that are being offered (e.g., one month's free rent), prices per square foot, utilities and services included in the rent (e.g., heat, hot water, shuttle bus service), and any upgrades or special features that are included in the sales price.
- Availability of subsidies to prospective renters or purchasers, plus the amount of the subsidies and the total number of units that can be subsidized.
- Vacancy rate or number of units remaining available for sale, and the characteristics of any waiting list for units.
- Any plans for additional development, and the anticipated timing of delivery of additional units.
- Amount of time required to lease or sell units, including the number of units sold or rented each month or each year.
- Renter or buyer profiles, and any comments addressing the most popular size, style, or type of unit.

Other planned and proposed new developments within the market area may also compete with the proposed project. Developers and operators of successful properties are quite likely to be considering another project; that information may emerge during discussions with them about their current properties. A related, probing question would be an inquiry on what they would do differently if they were starting over. Their answers may provide not only information on future competitive projects but also market insights that could be useful in refining the project concept or marketing plans of the development being analyzed.

## Reconciling Demand and Supply to Estimate Market Demand

Once information has been gathered from the various analyses, what is learned can be used to help the developer position the project in its market, determine the portions of the market demand that will be met by other existing and future housing developments, and estimate the portion of market demand that can be captured by the proposed development. Reaching conclusions about market position involves identifying one or more segments of demand that the project can tap, either as proposed or with realistic modifications. If the proposed development is not likely to be competitive, its market positioning should be changed, or the project should be scrapped.

The market positioning of the proposed development is determined by the kinds of households likely to be attracted to it and by the numbers of these households living in the primary and secondary housing market areas. For instance, demographic patterns may show an aging population, suggesting a potential demand for rental units targeted at empty nesters and senior citizens.

Where one or more market segments is growing in numbers of households, the process of reconciling demand and supply involves quantifying the growth, subtracting from it the units already in the market area that will meet the growth, and determining whether there is residual demand left over to be met by additional housing developments. For any given market segment or community, the process may be complicated by other factors, including location, proximity to services, unit size and design, and ethnic or racial concerns that must be factored into the analysis. And, as has been indicated, many potential segments of demand may have leveled off or declined in an inner-city housing market.

Positioning a development to respond successfully to the demand generated by a specific segment of the market may require the inclusion of special design features and amenities. For example, a review of demand by age may indicate that young single people are moving to the area; project design, amenities, and marketing would then be directed toward attracting that market segment. Young singles may be concerned about the security of an inner-city neighborhood, so a rental complex might install controlled entrances and secure off-street parking, as well as provide swimming pools and exercise facilities. Amenities offered by successful competitive projects with

## Figure 3.  Einstein Competitors

The following table exemplifies an inventory of comparable housing for seniors in a portion of the city of Philadelphia. The information was compiled as part of an analysis of the supply of subsidized housing for the elderly made in connection with a market analysis of a proposed new development. The data were assembled from the listings from two public agencies for seniors' housing operating in the city (no single, comprehensive listing existed), from visits to selected projects in the primary housing market area, and from telephone interviews with the managers of other properties in less competitive locations. From an initial, large table of comparable seniors' developments in Philadelphia, a smaller listing of competitive projects was identified, and a separate analysis compared the numbers of units in these properties with the demand for seniors' housing in the primary housing market area.

Because the properties are subsidized, rents have been based on the incomes of residents and driven by the requirements of the subsidy, rather than by the market. For this reason, rental rates have not been included in the table.

**Map of Einstein Competitors: Comparable Housing Projects for Seniors**

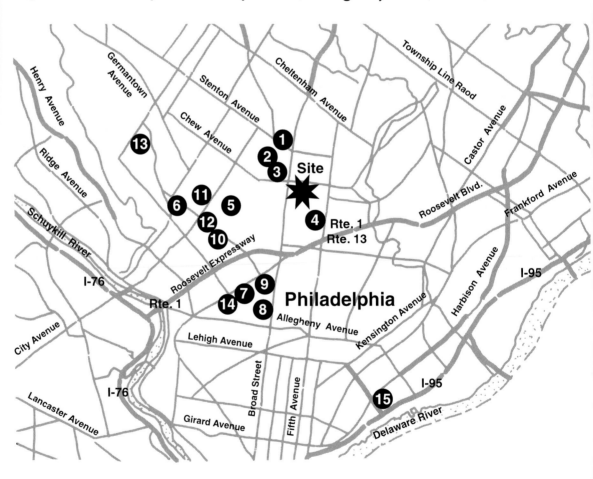

# A Survey of Comparable Very-Low-Income Properties Offering Seniors' Housing in Philadelphia

| Map No. | Project Name Address | Assistance Program | Number of Units | Bedroom Distribution | Vacant Units | Turnover | Waiting List | List Open/ Closed | Residents Drawn From | Amenities/ Services |
|---|---|---|---|---|---|---|---|---|---|---|
| 1 | Phillip Murray House 6300 Old York Rd. | Section 202 | 308 | Eff.: 210 (est) 1-BR: 98 (est) | 0 | NA | 2 years | Closed | Entire city | Not specified |
| 2 | Corinthian Square 6113 N. 21st St. | Section 202 | 60 | Eff.: 32 1-BR: 28 | 2 | Only on death | 100 (being reduced to 50) | Closed | Entire city | Independent living services |
| 3 | Kemble Park 5701 Ogontz Ave. | PHFA Section 8 | 50 total, with 16 elderly | NA | | | | | | |
| 4 | Philippian Gardens 8th & Lindlay Streets | Section 202 | 50 | Eff.: 13 1-BR: 37 | 0 | 1–2 per year | About 25 | Open | Logan section Entire city | Meals on Wheels, home care, social worker |
| 5 | Elders Place 53 East Wister St. | Section 202 | 47 | Eff.: 16 1-BR: 30 2-BR: 1 | 1 | 3–4 per year | About 120 | Open | Entire city | Independent living services |
| 6 | Four Freedoms House 6108 Morris Street | Section 202 | 282 | NA | 0 | About 36 per year | About 300 | Open | Germantown Roxborough | Services coordinator |
| 7 | Venango House 2104 West Venango | Section 8 | 105 total, 95 elderly | 1-BR: 84 2-BR: 21 | 0 0 | Only on death | About 500 (2–3 year wait) | Open | North Philadelphia | Resident services coordinator, visiting nurse, recreation |
| 8 | Tioga Presbyterian Apartments 1531 West Tioga St. | Section 202 | 113 | 1-BR: 113 | 0 | Opened 1/96 | About 50 | Open | North Philadelphia | Senior center |
| 9 | Opportunities Towers I/II 1727 W. Hunting Park | Section 202 | 325 | Eff.: 101 1-BR: 101 | 2 | | NA (now purging list) | Open | Entire city | Meals, housekeeping |
| 10 | Enon Tolland Apartments 245 West Queen St. | Section 236 | 65 | Eff.: 59 1 BR: 6 | 0 | 1–2 per year | 6 months | | Germantown | In-home services |
| 11 | Germantown Interfaith 14–20 West Chelten Ave. | Section 202 | 96 | Eff.: 24 1-BR: 72 | 0 | About 10 per year | About 15 per year | Open | Germantown | Social worker |
| | Philadelphia Housing Authority Specific PHA projects included in the totals: | Public housing | 1,481 | NA | 0 | NA | About 400 | Open | Entire city | Caseworker, lunch, service coordinator (Of PHA's elderly projects, Germantown House and Emlen Arms are in most demand.) |
| 12 | Germantown House | | 220 | NA | | | | | | |
| 13 | Emlen Arms | | 174 | NA | | | | | | |
| 14 | Plymouth Hall | | 70 | NA | | | | | | |
| 15 | Somerset Villas 200 E. Somerset St. | Section 202 | 99 | Eff.: 25 1-BR: 74 | 1 | | About 55 | Closed 1 year Opening 1/96 | North Philadelphia Port Richmond | Independent living services |
| Not on Map | Shalom Apartments and Arbor House 12003 Bustleton Avenue | Sections 8 & 202 | 269 | NA | 0 | | 1,000+ | Closed | Northeast Philadelphia | Social worker, nurse |

*Source:* Interviews conducted by Real Estate Strategies, Inc.

similar market positioning may suggest features that should be included in the proposed development.

Pricing of residential units is a major factor determining the market position of an inner-city housing development. Most households shopping for housing are concerned about the price per unit, in terms of the rent or monthly payment. It is more difficult in most inner-city hous-

ing markets to lease larger, higher-rent units than smaller units priced to compete with existing developments. Nevertheless, units that are too small can also be difficult to sell or rent. For example, studio apartments are difficult to rent in Detroit, even in attractive, well-located properties.

Interestingly, prospective home purchasers in inner-city neighborhoods often are more concerned about the amount of the monthly hous-

In these before-and-after photos of Summit Place in St. Paul, Minnesota, a side-by-side duplex was renovated to become a six-unit condominium.

ing payment than the actual sales price of a housing unit, a factor that has been particularly apparent with homeownership assistance programs in Cleveland. In these programs, purchasers compared monthly payments with the rents that they would be required to pay, and special financing programs that reduced the payments enhanced the sales pace of infill subdivisions in the city.

Positioning a proposed development in the market so that it can respond favorably to market demand is not always possible, even when the changes would improve the competitive market position of the development. When limits have been reached, market demand for the property must be assessed based on these limitations. If demand is insufficient, the project is not feasible.

## Estimating Capture Rates and Absorption

The capture rate is an estimate of the percentage of the demand that the individual project will attract. Thus, for a proposed development targeted at first-time buyers, the capture rate is the estimated percentage of all first-time buyers seeking units in the market area who will select that development. Estimates of capture rates usually are based on factors like the relative attractiveness of the development's location, design, types and sizes of units, price, quality, features, amenities, and other factors, compared with those available at other existing and planned developments.

An estimate of the likely rate of absorption—the number of units that will be rented or sold during a specified time frame, usually stated in months or years—is a critical component of financial feasibility because empty units do not generate cash flow. Thus, it is very important to estimate the amount of time that will be required before all units are rented or sold, as well as the carrying cost that must be budgeted to pay costs during the time frame from construction completion to full occupancy. For single-family houses, duplexes, and townhouses, it is possible to phase construction (assuming critical mass), based on estimates of absorption. For multifamily buildings and high rises for which construction phasing is not possible, however, it is important to be as realistic as possible about the number of units that can be absorbed within a specified time.

Barring a major change in the demand characteristics in an established market area, the recent experiences of developers of competitive projects, with appropriate adjustments to reflect market position, usually provide the best indications of the proposed project's likely absorption rate. Reviews of absorption rates must consider the number of properties and units being marketed at the same time to the same market segment. For example, a developer with a relatively slow absorption rate of two to three units per month may have been marketing the units while several competitive properties were also being offered. In estimating absorption for a future development, it is important to consider other planned developments that may become available while the subject development is being marketed.

It is important to remember that measures such as capture rate and absorption pace involve predictions about how a proposed development project will perform. At best, they are well-reasoned guesses by experienced market analysts. A project's actual performance will be affected by a wide range of unforeseeable factors, including future market conditions, the property's relative attractiveness, and how well it is marketed.

# Information Sources for Market Analysis

## Location Information

Government agencies are good sources of information on a particular location and the surrounding area. These agencies include local and regional planning departments, economic development organizations, redevelopment agencies, community development departments, housing finance agencies, and social service organizations.

In today's high-technology environment, it also is possible to obtain information about cities and their organization on the Internet. Cities and local chambers of commerce have home pages; cities that are participating in the Community Development Block Grant (CDBG) program of the Department of Housing and Urban Development (HUD) have consolidated plans that can be accessed on the Internet. Newspapers serving cities often can be found online, and recent articles on specific neighborhoods and planned developments, as well as reports of local development trends, can be accessed.

Local and regional planning departments typically are good sources of planning documents or studies, zoning maps, and other useful data and information. Representatives of planning agencies usually can identify sources that have census data for the city, as well as any local or regional studies that may be useful, and these representatives have, or know how to obtain, community maps and aerial photographs. Planners also can be helpful in describing local redevelopment plans, together with any highway,

street, and infrastructure improvements that may affect demand for an inner-city housing development. Community and economic development agencies often have their own development projects, proposed or ongoing, that will have an effect on an inner-city housing development, and these agency projects should be identified.

## Competitive Projects

Local development agencies can be good sources of information on existing, planned, and proposed housing developments in a city and can be helpful in identifying other resources that exist in the project area. For instance, there may be a directory of community-based organizations that can be obtained, listings of building permits and planning approvals that have been granted for projects that may compete with the subject development when they have been completed, and/or listings of subsidized housing projects in the city.

## Development Process and Regulations

Local officials can provide information about development processes and procedures, including parking and lot coverage requirements and height limitations that may affect the development and its timing. In addition, they can be sources of information about environmental or historic preservation issues, e.g., the locations of flood-prone areas, "brownfield" problems, the boundaries of a historic district that may affect the proposed development, and historic preservation issues or

concerns. Finally, it often is possible to ascertain whether there will be support for the proposed housing development by interviewing government representatives who will be responsible for development approvals later on in the process and who will communicate with the developer or sponsor if there are any problems or concerns.

## Economic Information

Data for the economic analysis can be obtained from U.S. government sources, economic reporting and forecasting firms, state and local agencies, and online data services that provide economic and demographic data. Although issues will vary depending on the area and on general economic conditions, the data assembled will address economic trends, employment and major employers, workforce characteristics, population and household growth, household income characteristics, and age patterns.

U.S. government agencies and economic forecasting firms provide data on key regional economic trends: growth in gross metropolitan product, employment growth, unemployment rate, personal income growth, and related data. Most state departments of labor also report routinely on labor force and employment characteristics, and these data are available at the city and county level, often broken out by economic sector. Planning and economic development departments and chambers of commerce in most cities can supply information on how to obtain relevant data if they themselves are not able to provide this information. These sources also usually have listings of major employers, including information on employment levels in the city.

## Demographic Data

Demographic and employment data for cities, counties, and metropolitan areas from the most recent U.S. Census are available from a range of sources, including publications in public libraries. The U.S. Department of Commerce's Bureau of the Census also has made large volumes of data available online through the Internet, which can be accessed directly. Labor and employment data are available online, and CD-ROM data files may be purchased at reasonable prices. Other sources of economic and demographic data include regional planning agencies, chambers of commerce, state and local colleges and universities, and public libraries with good reference departments.

Several online data services also make demographic data available quickly for specified geographic areas, which may be as small as postal zip codes or census tracts. In addition to data from the 1990 Census, these services also provide current-year estimates and five-year projections of demographic data that can be very useful in looking prospectively at housing markets.

Demographic patterns and trends can be obtained by using data only from the U.S. Bureau of the Census for 1980 and 1990, but many market analysts today tap online data services that provide small-area data

for census tracts and postal zip codes from the most recent census, as well as estimates for the current year and five-year projections. Baseline census data, estimates, and projections that are useful in measuring demand for housing include information on: the population in the housing market areas and the extent to which the population has grown and is projected to grow; numbers of households, and trends showing patterns of growth or decline in these numbers; numbers of households by age, race, sex, and ethnicity; and household income and wealth.

Of particular interest is a cross-tabulation that yields information on the numbers of households by age of the head of household, by income bracket. This "age-by-income" tabulation is very useful in analyzing the number of households in various age brackets that relate to the type of housing that may be desirable, such as the total number of households aged 25 to 34 years, and/or the number with incomes sufficient to become first-time homebuyers. Similarly, age-by-income tabuations will show demand for subsidized seniors' housing through data on households headed by individuals 65 years old and older who have limited incomes. For seniors' households, special tabulations of data give additional information on the incomes of elderly households within different age bands, the numbers of owners and renters, household characteristics, and physical and care limitations.

Although the data produced by online proprietary data ser-

vices are very helpful in identifying population and household trends and in estimating demand, it is important in using these data to remember that estimates are just that: estimates made by using the best procedures currently available to update the most recent U.S. Census. Estimates are more reliable for larger geographic areas; hence, those for the United States are likely to be more accurate than, say, those for a particular city or for market areas that may be established within a city. Moreover, all projections are by their very nature predictions of events that will occur in the future. As such, they are subject to error, and margins of error in estimates and projections increase as the geographic area becomes smaller.

Because many inner-city neighborhoods are declining in population and in numbers of households, it is also important to note that it is more difficult to measure a declining population or a rapidly growing population than it is to measure a moderately growing one. And the difficulty is compounded by the problems with undercounts of inner-city populations that reportedly occurred in the 1990 Census!

For many cities, regional planning organizations, state agencies, universities, and other public agencies develop their own projections of population and households, and it is useful to compare estimates that have been developed by different sources before reaching conclusions. Another highly useful source of data for both demand and supply analyses is the American Housing Survey, which gathers data on population and housing characteristics for specified metropolitan areas each year. The surveys, which are conducted by the Census Bureau, provide data for specified city jurisdictions within a metropolitan area, although not for smaller market areas within cities.

## Existing Housing Supply

To gather information on the general characteristics of the supply of existing housing in a defined market area or areas, data from the most recent U.S. Census are a good starting point, and published data, as well as online services, can be used to obtain information on the number of owner-occupied units, rental units, and vacant units at the time of the census. Census data also include rents charged for rental units and estimates of housing value for owner-occupied units. Online data services provide housing data by census tract and zip code and also estimate and project housing value and numbers of housing units.

## Area Housing Condition

Walks in the neighborhood, talks with housing managers, and talks with local residents are the best sources of qualitative and impressionistic information. Quantitative measures of housing condition are more difficult to find, unless a recent local study has been conducted. Baseline U.S. Census data address only the number of housing units lacking plumbing or kitchens, and very few dwelling units today have such deficien-

cies—usually less than 1 percent of the dwelling units in a large city.

Where there has been a recent American Housing Survey, data usually are available for the center city and for the metropolitan area on the number of units with selected deficiencies, such as leaking roofs, exterior and interior cracks, and exposed wiring.

Another potential source of general information on housing condition is the local administrator of Section 8 existing housing and voucher programs. Officials responsible for inspections of units to determine compliance with housing quality standards often can comment on the extent to which units in an area comply with the standards and on whether major problems with housing conditions exist. But beyond such gross measures, the market analyst usually must make judgments about the general condition of housing in the market area on the basis only of interviews and observations.

## For-Sale Housing Supply

Interviews with realtors usually provide a wealth of information on home sales in the market area, and if they are willing to be helpful, local real estate sales representatives can tap multiple-listing service data on recent sales, along with descriptions of current listings. If local realtors cannot be enlisted to help, a more time-consuming process is to review property transfer records at city hall or the county courthouse.

In addition, data on the number of property transfers

annually and on average sales prices can be purchased from companies that specialize in compiling the data, and they often are available at the postal zip-code level.

Other good sources of information are developers and sales representatives of properties recently sold or currently for sale in the market area.

## Rental Housing Supply

Property management companies are good sources of information on existing rental housing. In many communities, a few property management companies may handle large numbers of rental properties in a specific market area, and interviews with representatives of these companies can build a solid base of data on occupancy rates, renter profiles, rent levels, and desirable amenities.

On Capitol Hill in Washington, D.C., for example, three property management companies handle a very large percentage of the units offered for rent in the market area, and interviews with representatives can yield valuable information on rents, market conditions, and trends. In other cities, more extensive research is required, and many more interviews must be conducted to understand the nature of the existing supply and the effect that it will have on the proposed development.

# Santa Ana Pines, Watts, Los Angeles, California

Santa Ana Pines was the first new single-family development built in the Watts section of Los Angeles in many years.

The experience of Santa Ana Pines demonstrates how the requirements attached to different sources of financing can limit the potential market and can erect barriers to project success.

Santa Ana Pines is a development of 114 two-story, detached, market-rate houses on 13.7 acres in the Watts section of Los Angeles. Developed by The Williams/Greer Group, the project was conceived in 1989, with the purchase of land from the Southern Pacific Railroad. Construction began in 1991 and continues today.

The development gives moderate-income households the first opportunity to purchase a new single-family house in this community since 1985. The Spanish-style homes, designed by Jones & Martinez, feature textured stucco exteriors, concrete tile roofs, two-car garages, landscaped yards, and secluded patios with gas grills.

The project was financed by a group of private investors. Wells Fargo Bank funded the construction. The city has provided soft seconds through its Community Redevelopment Agency and Community Development Block Grant funds, plus a takeout of the construction loan through the sale of mortgage revenue bonds. The original plan was to develop ten phases of ten to 14 homes each. Three phases have been built, but after the third phase, the interest carry on the land became difficult. The city loaned the developer money to pay off the land loan from Wells Fargo Bank. The developer sold the last three phases of the project to Habitat for Humanity and bought out the project's other investors.

Home prices within a three-mile radius of the site average $100,000. In Santa Ana Pines, house prices averaged $150,000 in the first phase, $155,000 in the second phase, and $165,000 in the third. The typical buyer is a two- or three-worker household from the local area that is buying a first home. Thirty-six houses have been built; 44 remain for future phases of development; and 32 were sold to Habitat for Humanity. Two lots are zoned for commercial development.

Sales have slowed, as buyer income restrictions associated with the financing have resulted in a very narrow band of prospective buyers. (To be eligible for purchase, buyers can make no more than 80 percent of the area median income; yet to qualify for a loan based on city-provided soft seconds, buyers must make at least 72 to 75 percent of the area median income, have a good credit history, and have saved enough money—$3,000 to $4,000—to pay the required upfront costs.) As a result, the developer is renegotiating with the city.

# Garibaldi Square, Chicago, Illinois

In the Garibaldi Square development in Chicago, garage townhouses surround an inviting public gathering space.

The success of Garibaldi Square shows that a well-designed residential development can attract middle-income, market-rate buyers to a transitional urban neighborhood.

Garibaldi Square is a high-density urban residential community on six and one-half acres just west of downtown Chicago. Eighty-six fee-simple townhouses and 42 condominiums combine suburban-style amenities such as open, public greenspace and private garages with urban design elements consistent with the surrounding Victorian rowhouses. Low land costs made it possible to offer the homes at affordable prices.

Charles H. Shaw, chairman of The Shaw Company, a respected Chicago mixed-use development firm, had three goals in developing this residential community. He wanted the project to be financially successful. He wanted to work closely with active community groups to ensure that the project was compatible with and enhanced the existing urban fabric. And finally, he hoped that the development would spur additional investment and improvements in the area.

To draw the desired middle- and upper-income homebuyers, The Shaw Company knew it had to deliver a high-quality, attractive product at a competitive price. Because land costs were reasonable, the developers were able to relax the densities and provide amenities that are uncommon in urban housing. This combination, as well as a product mix that appealed to a broad market, contributed greatly to the project's success.

## The Site

Garibaldi Square is located just two miles from the heart of downtown Chicago, at the intersection of West Harrison Street and South Ashland Avenue in University Village. University Village is a traditionally Italian neighborhood on Chicago's West Side that had come to include a broad racial mix. The site, located next to a park that contains a statue of the Italian leader Garibaldi, was a highly visible but unappealing tract of land. But because it was situated between Rush Presbyterian St. Luke's Medical Center and the University of Illinois at Chicago, the proposed site, which had been vacant for many years, had the potential to arrest the decline of this historic neighborhood.

The site was acquired by the city of Chicago in the late 1960s and cleared as part of the city's urban renewal program. In the 1970s, The Shaw Company obtained an option to buy the land from the city for about $1 per square foot. To complete the land assembly, a land swap was arranged with the board of education, exchanging the critical northwestern corner parcel of the site for a site across West Harrison Street. Through the land swap, The Shaw Company obtained complete control of the entire site, while the board of education gained a site for a new magnet school that would further enhance the vitality of the neighborhood.

## Planning and Design

The Shaw Company invited a suburban residential developer, Home by Hemphill, to co-develop townhouses for the site. With the architectural firm Nagle, Hartray & Associates, the developers took care to design new houses that were comparable to the existing houses in size, scale, and design so that they blended in well with their surroundings yet created a visually identifiable development with a distinctive architectural style. A second design goal was to offer suburban amenities such as open greenspace, off-street parking, and a high level of security, all in a distinctly urban style. And finally, the developers sought to develop a high-quality product with top-of-the-market features that could be sold at a favorable price. The sales price had to represent a good value for the buyer when compared with similar homes in other city neighborhoods or in surrounding suburbs.

The project was developed in three phases: Phase I consisted of 48 three-story townhouses; Phase II included a total of 38 townhouses in two locations on the site; and Phase III was composed of 42 condominium units, designed as first-floor garden apartments with two-story townhomes above.

To create a community within a community, some homes are clustered along driving courts parallel to Harrison Street. Others form a crescent that faces inward toward a court that contains a central lawn with a fountain and public seating, providing a sense of community and exclusivity for the residents. The townhouses' design —three stories with a mix of pitched and flat roofs—strongly echoes that of the Victorian and turn-of-the-century buildings in the neighborhood. All are built of red brick with limestone-trimmed facades and colored window frames. The condominiums feature the same materials and compatible architecture but offer a more moderate-priced home choice.

Each townhome has a garage on the entry level with access directly into the home. Parking for the condominiums is provided in a covered, secured garage directly adjacent to the units. This garage, which is partially submerged, has colored gravel designs on its roof to offer a more pleasing view from residents' windows. Other security features include wrought-iron fencing, limited access into the development, and specially designed lighting.

## Financing and Sales

The project was financed with a conventional loan from Continental Bank, with end-loan commitments purchased by the developer from several major financial institutions. There were no buydowns of mortgages, and many of the purchasers found financing independently of these commitments. A temporary problem arose when early appraisals came in too low to support the necessary loan amounts because of the absence of comparable properties in the area. But the properties were reassessed at more realistic amounts, and this single obstacle to financing was eliminated.

Sales were brisk from the beginning, and the project sold out in three years. More than half of the homebuyers were from other city neighborhoods, about 20 percent came from the suburbs, and another 21 percent from the immediate neighborhood. The remaining six buyers came from out of state. Fewer than 20 percent (22 buyers) were associated with the university or medical center. While a significant majority (91 purchasers) were in the 30- to 50-year age group, only 20 percent of all purchasers had children.

By developing an upscale project next to the medical center, the developers also generated additional value for the surrounding property, much of which is owned by the medical center. Moreover, the Inn at University Village, a hotel owned by the medical center, was built in conjunction with Garibaldi Square. The inn offers lodging and other services to meet the increasing demand for outpatient medical care, meeting rooms, and other amenities for visitors and families of patients and visiting personnel.

## Experience Gained

- New residential developments can succeed in marginal urban areas if the developer and the community can wait until the market is ready to absorb the product and if a high-quality product can be offered at a highly competitive price. (Very low land costs help make competitive pricing possible.)

- Developments in established communities, especially in the inner city, can succeed only if they are done in consultation and coordination with existing neighborhood organizations.
- Projects that involve the reuse of urban sites can present special problems with regard to demolition, debris removal, and the installation of sewer and water services. Builders should plan to remove no more than is absolutely necessary, even to the point of creating grade rather than removing old foundations or other obstacles. A soils engineer should be part of the planning and development team from the outset.
- The attractiveness and marketability of a project can be strengthened with design variations. Though developers may view these refinements as significant cost factors, they can often be added at little additional overall expense. The project architect must know how to use them most effectively, and construction supervision must be vigilant to ensure that design variations are carried out properly and in the most cost-efficient manner.

## Garibaldi Square Project Data

### Land Use Information

Site Area: 6.5 acres
Total Dwelling Units: 128
Gross Density: 19.7 units/acre
Total Parking Spaces: 252
  Uncovered: 108
  Covered: 144
Maximum Number of Stories: 3

### Land Use Plan

| | Acres | Percent of Site |
|---|---|---|
| Buildings | 1.89 | 29 |
| Parking Areas | 0.26 | 4 |
| Roads/Driveways | 1.17 | 18 |
| Landscaped Areas | 3.18 | 49 |
| Total | 6.50 | 100 |

### Development Cost Information

| | Total | Percent of Costs |
|---|---|---|
| Site Acquisition Cost | $ 390,000 | 1.5 |
| Site Improvement Cost | 1,528,000 | 6.1 |
| Construction Costs | 19,142,000 | 75.9 |
| Soft Costs | | |
| Sales | 573,000 | |
| Marketing | 302,000 | |
| Models | 121,000 | |
| Architect | 181,000 | |
| Taxes | 192,000 | |
| Insurance | 122,000 | |
| Accounting | 27,000 | |
| Legal | 225,000 | |
| General/administrative | 350,000 | |
| Project | 1,211,000 | |
| Finance | 297,000 | |
| Interest | 465,000 | |
| Warranty reserve | 104,000 | |
| Total | 4,170,000 | 16.5 |
| Total Project Costs | $25,230,000 | 100.0 |

### Residential Unit Information

| Type | Living Area (Square Feet) | No. of Units | Sales Price (Starting/Final) |
|---|---|---|---|
| Fee-Simple Townhouses | | | |
| 2-bedroom/2-car | 1,652 | 16 | $158,900/$197,900 |
| | 1,774 | | 168,900/204,900 |
| 3-bedroom/1-car | 2,124 | 35 | 201,900/227,900 |
| | 2,136 | | 223,900/234,900 |
| | 2,220 | | 228,900/234,900 |
| 3-bedroom/loft/1-car | 2,257 | 19 | 209,900/239,900 |
| | 2,271 | | 224,900/249,900 |
| 3-bedroom/2-car | 1,880 | 4 | 234,900/244,900 |
| 3-bedroom/loft/2-car | 2,102 | 12 | 207,900/224,900 |
| Total | | 86 | |
| Condominium Apartments | | | |
| 2-bedroom flat | 912 | 12 | $114,900/$129,900 |
| 3-bedroom townhouse | 1,529 | 12 | 165,900/188,900 |
| 2-bedroom flat on park | 912 | 9 | 124,900/129,900 |
| 3-bedroom townhouse/ loft | 1,793 | 9 | 185,900/209,900 |
| Total | | 42 | |

Source: ULI Project Reference File report, Volume 22, Number 10.

# Siena at Renaissance Park, Atlanta, Georgia

Siena at Renaissance Park demonstrates how offering good value to a carefully targeted market can lead to project success.

The project consists of 52 condominium units contained within three buildings that are sited around a formal courtyard on a 2.7-acre urban infill site in Atlanta. Hard costs totaled approximately $52 per square foot, and the units sold (in 1989) for prices ranging from $73,300 to $145,000. The project offered three basic floor plans: one-bedroom/one-bath units with den; two-bedroom/two-bath units; and double master-suite units, several of which also contained a loft den.

Siena at Renaissance Park sold quickly in an otherwise languishing residential market through careful attention to buyers' preferences, as well as through a unique combination of financial factors that permitted monthly payments at Siena to be lower than the rent for apartments of comparable quality and space.

## The Site

The project is located within the Bedford-Pine urban redevelopment area, which was cleared in the 1960s. Convinced of the viability of the downtown community, Ackerman & Company bought 30 acres of land in Bedford-Pine in 1980. The company's first projects were a 28-unit townhouse condominium project and a 56-unit, stacked-flat condominium proj-

ect, located immediately to the west and north of the site respectively. Concurrently with the Siena project, Ackerman developed a 192-unit apartment complex. Ackerman's most recent addition to the area is RIO, an innovative 15,000-square-foot restaurant and specialty retail center packed with custom landscape features and artistic detailing.

These projects, together with several by other developers, have helped the area to achieve a critical mass as a desirable residential location. Local city parks offer lighted tennis courts and other recreational facilities. Downtown Atlanta, two MARTA rapid-rail stations to the

west, and community landmarks such as the Fox Theatre in the redeveloping midtown neighborhood to the north are all within walking distance.

## Planning and Design

Architect Niles Bolton Associates (NBA) designed the project with classical architectural references reminiscent of houses that were built in Atlanta at the turn of the century. The three residential buildings relate to one another in a formal arrangement around a parklike courtyard. Richly landscaped grounds are accentuated with fountains and ornamental lighting. All parking is at grade, and an elegant

Siena at Renaissance Park, Ackerman & Company's community of metropolitan condominium homes, was the first intown housing project developed in midtown Atlanta.

37

wrought-iron fence bounds the perimeter of the site. An electronic gate on Renaissance Parkway secures the single point of vehicular access.

With eight units on each full floor, the buildings employ an adaptation of a traditional breezeway floor plan; however, the entryways are enclosed and carpeted and feature soaring cathedral ceilings. The buildings are wood-frame construction with lightweight concrete floors and a stucco and brick exterior. Batt insulation was installed between floors for sound control.

All units offer fireplaces, nine-foot ceilings, tray ceilings in formal dining rooms, ceramic-tiled foyers, oversized windows, and an outdoor deck or patio. Custom options, the availability of which was critical for selling to the design-conscious target market, accounted for 150 modifications to the original construction contract. A central recreational facility, including a pool, spa, and clubhouse, was constructed during a separate second phase—a 120-unit project northwest of the Phase I site. A third phase was also completed.

## Financing

A tax exemption was made possible through a state Residential Urban Enterprise Act, which eliminates for five years all property taxes except bonded indebtedness and sanitation charges in special zones established by city and county gov-ernments. Property taxes are phased in during years six through 10 at 20 percent per year. This program resulted in tax savings to condominium buyers for the first five years ranging from $120 to $200 per month.

Low-interest financing was obtained through the city's Urban Residential Finance Authority, which provides tax-exempt, bond-issue mortgage funds to condominium buyers at 30-year fixed rates of 8.9 percent, with a 2-to-1 buydown available at a starting rate of 6.9 percent. The developer, Ackerman & Company, paid 4.7 points toward acquisition and obtained the commitment for financing from a local company. As this program involved a minimum downpayment of only 5 percent, practically all purchasers took advantage of it.

## Marketing

Ackerman marketed the project primarily to young, single professionals working in the downtown. More than 35 percent of the units were presold when the project opened in February 1989; the remaining units sold within an additional five months. Ackerman commissioned a marketing survey to determine what the residents liked and disliked about their homes and services. With dinner for two at a local restaurant offered as an incentive for completed surveys returned by a given date, the response rate to the four-page survey was 75 per-cent. The results of the survey were used to refine the plans for the project's second phase.

## Experience Gained

- Higher-density residential projects place greater demands on design in terms of quality, privacy, and access.
- Although demand for residential units in intown locations, close to urban amenities and workplaces, is strong among young, single professionals, this market is generally difficult to reach through the media. A more effective marketing strategy is to encourage personal referrals by offering existing owners a referral fee of $500.
- Do not lose sight of what the market can afford. The key to this project's success was finding the price point for those interested in living intown. Because the target market was young, single professionals with incomes between $25,000 and $45,000, base prices were kept as low as possible, and custom features were offered at additional cost.
- During the construction period, the presence of a staffed reception center in an on-site trailer enhanced sales; a significant number of purchasers were introduced to the project as drive-bys.

*Source:* Excerpted and updated from *ULI Project Reference File* report, Volume 20, Number 10.

## CHAPTER 3

# Developing in Inner-City Environments

**W**hile the basic process for developing infill housing is similar to that followed for other types of housing, a number of considerations are specific to housing developments undertaken in inner-city environments. Developers who are considering infill sites must be alert to certain kinds of site-specific problems, inadequacies in infrastructure, problems with land acquisition and assembly, difficult neighborhood environments, more stringent regulatory constraints, and, typically, the need to piece together a financing strategy from a number of public and private sources. These potential problems can be especially vexing when developing small projects, which cannot benefit from economies of scale and do not receive much attention or assistance from the public sector.

## Site Selection and Acquisition

One of the advantages of developing housing in central cities is the availability of parcels of vacant and underused land and buildings at the center of a metropolitan region. Land for infill development can range from individual building lots to plots for large-scale development resulting from, for example, tracts that have been assembled and cleared by earlier urban renewal projects, surplus land owned by institutions (churches, universities, or hospitals), public lands (excess land acquired for transportation facilities or former military installations), or defunct golf courses and country clubs.

As for any real estate development, factors to be considered in evaluating the suitability of a site for infill housing development include loca-tion, access, topography, vistas, drainage, availability of utilities, existing and future zoning, and the size and shape of the property in relation to the number of housing units proposed.

### Physical Characteristics of the Site

In making an evaluation, it is important to remember that sites that have been passed over for development or have not been redeveloped for another use are generally idle for a reason. A site might be too small or oddly shaped. Unstable soils, steep slopes, poor drainage, or vulnerability to flooding could make development infeasible. Street access might be a problem.

Inner-city sites usually have had some type of structure on them at one time, and it is important to inquire about the type of structure and whether soil borings have been completed. Residential structures that previously stood on the property may have had basements, and the rubble from the demolition may have been used to fill the previously excavated area. Previously developed sites might contain buried debris or unusable foundations or infrastructure. Old utility sites may traverse the site in unmapped locations. Interim uses such as parking lots might need to be removed.

Trinity Development Associates, during development of the Trinity Court infill townhouse project in Yonkers, New York, found that it had to break up and remove the foundations of earlier structures, which meant an unexpected expense and delay. K. Hovnanian Companies, while developing a 600-unit stacked townhouse project, Society Hill at University Heights in Newark, New Jersey, discovered that the site contained concrete, stone, bricks, and asphalt left from old foundations, streets, sidewalks, and curbs. The firm's response was to pulverize these materials on site and to recycle them into needed new roads and parking lots.

Perhaps the most troublesome of potential site problems is the possibility of environmental contamination, which can increase a project's risk, cost, and complexity. If the former residence used oil heat, the tank may have leaked and contaminated the soil, or it may still be buried on the site. Prior use of the property for industrial purposes may mean that the property has some environmental contamination that must be contained or removed. The discovery of toxic or hazardous substances on a site can necessitate potentially expensive removal or remediation and can pose liability and insurance problems for the landowner as well. Asbestos or lead contamination in older buildings can make rehabilitation projects economically infeasible. Developers must evaluate infill sites carefully to identify these kinds of problems before committing to the purchase of a site.

## The Optimal Infill Site

### The Context
- Viable market.
- Compatible, well-maintained surrounding properties.
- Receptive neighborhood.
- Helpful city government.
- Workable building code.
- Good public services.

### The Property
- Availability for sale at a realistic price.
- Sufficient size for intended use(s).
- Adequate utilities in place.
- Street frontage.
- Regularly shaped, developable parcels.
- No major topographic, drainage, or subsoil problems.
- Appropriate zoning.
- Potential development profitability, compared with alternative sites.

Source: Real Estate Research Corporation, *Infill Development Strategies* (Washington, D.C.: Urban Land Institute and American Planning Association (1982, out of print), p. 11.

Existing structures on the site may present interesting and unusual opportunities for rehabilitation and reuse, but these structures must be carefully inspected and evaluated to make sure that the desired rehabilitation is possible within a workable development budget and that the structures can be modified or adapted to meet today's residential standards. In particular, requirements associated with historic preservation or with managing environmental hazards such as asbestos or lead-based paint may add significantly to development costs.

### Visibility, Travel Considerations, and Infrastructure

The selected site must have good visibility and street access, as well as access to major roadways and transportation systems. A location near a major highway sometimes is a detriment to residential development because of the noise and unsightly vistas. On the other hand, visibility from a major highway can contribute positively to marketing a residential development, and good access to major thoroughfares connecting to employment centers can be a competitive advantage for a proposed development. In some cases, however, highways can also act as barriers: in many low-income, inner-city neighborhoods, the community is separated from the downtown or from more attractive parts of the city by a limited-access highway.

An important consideration is how potential residents will travel from the proposed development to places of employment, shopping, and services. Issues include the convenience of roadways, travel time to employment centers, and the types of neighborhoods that residents will pass through on their way to and from the development. Access to public transportation should be considered, as well as whether transit routes provide direct service to employment centers or require one or more transfers. If it will be necessary to walk to a transit station or stop, an assessment of the walking route should be included in the analysis.

Proximity to services, employment centers, and amenities, plus the quality of the facilities and services that will be available to residents, are important considerations in assessing the site and environment of an inner-city housing development.

The relative ease or difficulty of shopping for food, medicines, clothing, and other necessities must be considered in evaluating the location of a proposed inner-city housing development. Hav-

The Homan Square site, located on a 55-acre former Sears headquarters site in Chicago's North Lawndale neighborhood, contains the original Sears Tower—the visual symbol of the community.

ing groceries and drugstores nearby is especially important to seniors, who often do not have automobiles or are not comfortable driving to shopping centers. Although some retailers have discovered the buying power that exists in inner-city neighborhoods, many such communities still have few modern retail stores offering a reasonable variety of high-quality goods at acceptable prices. Local officials and community-based organizations can advise on whether any new retailing is proposed in the vicinity.

The presence of existing infrastructure is often cited as a motivation for developing infill sites, but in some cases, the infrastructure might be ill maintained or insufficient to meet today's design standards. In many inner-city neighborhoods, existing infrastructure needs to be repaired, replaced, or modernized to serve both existing and new development. The cost of needed improvements can sometimes be prohibitive.

## Considerations in Buying the Land

Acquiring the land for infill housing development in city neighborhoods can be challenging because of the size and configuration of available parcels, ownership problems (unclear titles, absentee owners who are difficult to find, tax liens, speculation), and price, which in some locations may be too high to enable marketable developments.

Speculation can result in surprisingly high land prices in inner-city neighborhoods, and the timing of land acquisition can be tricky. Depending on the properties' locations and holding costs,

owners may retain them, pricing the properties above market in anticipation of an eventual rise in value—especially if there is other development or public improvement occurring or expected in the area.

Because developments in inner-city neighborhoods often must be large enough to signal a significant change in the character of the community, it may be necessary to acquire land from several owners. Once landowners become aware that property is being purchased, prices for the remaining parcels rise quickly. So it would seem wise to acquire as much land as possible early in the process. Yet carrying costs are high; to make a profit, a developer must begin development soon after acquiring the land.

Land in city neighborhoods must compete for development with comparatively inexpensive suburban land, which benefits from subsidized highway construction, the public's willingness to commute, and comparatively lower local taxes. Infill sites in established neighborhoods generally are more expensive to acquire and develop than raw land. In the suburbs, a developer can often provide a larger house for the same price, in part because "infill projects are usually smaller but have the same amount of overhead, toxic cleanup costs can be high, parking is more expensive to provide, the number of units produced is generally lower than [for] suburban projects[, and] the permit costs are about the same."[1]

According to ULI member Mike Meyer, managing partner of E&Y Kenneth Leventhal Real Estate

Group in Newport Beach, California, infill development can still be a good niche for small local developers. Sources of information on infill sites are highly fragmented, and local knowledge—for instance, of school closings—gives local developers the edge in finding the best sites. Other sites can be found by envisioning alternate uses for a vacant or underused site. Although infill sites can be extremely profitable, many are small, and the overhead costs to acquire and develop a small infill site can be significant. Nevertheless, small to medium-sized builders with local knowledge can compete with large, publicly traded builders for these sites.

## Neighborhood Environment

In selecting an infill location, developers should consider the character of the surrounding neighborhood and what other developments or public actions are planned to revitalize and maintain the neighborhood.

Infill parcels in urban neighborhoods are often sited in districts characterized by high rates of poverty, low property values, crime, and drugs, where it has been difficult to attract new investment and where living can be a challenge. For this reason, it is essential that the city be committed to helping to create a more attractive living and investment environment to support infill housing developments in distressed neighborhoods. (For ways in which cities can help, see Chapter 6.)

In focus groups conducted for Chicago's City-Homes program by Applied Real Estate Analysis, participants were asked what kinds of houses they wanted. In response, they said they must first have confidence in the neighborhood. Before they risk their money investing in a neighborhood, they want to see public investment and amenities and to feel confident that their properties would appreciate.

Especially for families with children, the quality of the public schools is an issue—often, the issue that determines where they live—and in city neighborhoods, the quality of local schools is often poor. If the public schools are perceived as ineffective or, worse yet, as dangerous, middle-income people will not choose to locate in the center city. As Professor Joseph Gyourko of the University of Pennsylvania has been quoted as saying, "A declining educational system will overwhelm anything real estate can do."[2] In many cities, well-researched market analyses predict that the market for residential units will include few households with school-age children, and these analyses recommend targeting childless singles and couples, empty nesters, and elderly households.

Regardless of the age and income of potential residents, security is a key issue. Safety and security are emotional issues, and even if statistics can be gathered to show that there is not a problem, perceptions affect demand and must be considered in assessing the market for the inner-city housing units proposed.

The physical environment—the condition of streets, sidewalks, public areas, and nearby structures, and the nature of nearby land uses—is also important in determining the desirability of a neighborhood and the marketability of a project. The quality and frequency of public services is important, too.

To attract the potential market to transitional or distressed neighborhoods, residential or mixed-use developments must be of sufficient magnitude to exert some control over the neighborhood environment, to make visible improvements, and to engender confidence in the neighborhood's future. Large-scale projects with substantial support from the public sector, such as Quality Hill in Kansas City and Homan Square in Chicago, can greatly help to transform the character and image of a distressed neighborhood and to stimulate further investment.

According to Richard Baron, president of McCormack Baron & Associates of St. Louis, the threshold number of units for critical mass is about 200 units. In addition, in developing Westminster Place, Baron "reclaimed as much land as quickly as possible so that the development appeared larger in scale." This strategy reinforced the perception that the area was indeed changing and helped inspire confidence that it was becoming a new and better neighborhood.

Knowledgeable developers of inner-city housing developments often focus on sites near the edge of an area requiring revitalization, rather than ones that have blight surrounding them on all sides or that would require potential residents to travel along streets marked by deterioration to reach a new housing development. As Winston Folkers, a Cincinnati developer, has noted, in economically desirable areas, infill housing will take place spontaneously. In depressed areas, infill development cannot begin in the middle of the neighborhood; it must start at the edges and work in.

## Community Involvement

Contacts with community-based organizations can be valuable in helping to understand the dynamics of the neighborhood and the concerns of neighborhood residents. Experience has shown that communications with community-based organizations are an essential part of inner-city housing development; the sooner the process begins, the more likely it is that any problems will be identified and addressed.

When any infill development is proposed for an established neighborhood, existing residents may object, even if the development will improve the neighborhood. It is important to understand and consider the groups' positions on the development that is proposed and the reasons for their positions. Existing residents may fear gentrification, displacement, and change; they may want to preserve any vacant property as open space; they may be concerned that community facilities will be overloaded by the influx of newcomers; and they may be concerned about the quality, appearance, and spillover effects (such as on-street parking) of the proposed development. In many areas, neighborhood residents can recite a history of unfulfilled promises, and as a result, they do not trust developers or the government.

Neighboring communities will often object, either directly or indirectly, to any development that includes lower-income households. For example, in one city, opposition to a proposed housing development was motivated in part by a belief that a proposed mixed-income development would not attract higher-income residents and would ultimately become a concentration of low-income, minority households, thus adversely affecting property values.

In working with surrounding neighborhoods, developer Joseph Corcoran, president of Corcoran Jennison Companies of Boston, finds that the best approach is to show the neighbors other projects that the firm has completed so they can see what the projects look like, how they work, and what can be expected.

Some developers avoid the hassle by choosing to develop only where their projects are welcomed or even initiated by the local community. "Community support is essential," notes Richard Baron. "I have no interest in trying to convince a city. I only go to communities where there is a stated interest in seeing things change—where I'm invited to come in to solve a problem." Being able to count on city support enables the developer to focus time, money, and energy on developing the project, rather than on fighting political battles.

To avoid problems from the community, the basic rule is "Never 'blindside' the neighbors."[3] Developers should involve neighborhood groups early in the development process, keep them informed, hear their concerns, and actively listen to their suggestions regarding what kind of development is needed and desired. As a result of early and ongoing dialogue, existing residents can often be transformed into advocates for the proposed development, especially when "new projects can become part of the solution to old problems that have long disturbed existing residents."[4]

## Regulatory Process

In general, government regulation of infill development tends to be more demanding and costly than new development in newly developing places, and experienced infill developers allow extra time—and budget—to navigate the approvals process. "The preference of most developers to build on raw land is less a product of market demand than of costs and opportunities, many of them directly imposed by local government policies."[5]

Rezoning is often required. Many infill parcels are zoned for uses that have become economically infeasible. In single-family districts, for instance, developers may need to build multifamily housing to offset the higher land costs and to make a profit. In addition, building codes designed for new construction may be unrealistic for rehabilitation projects, and restrictions on use can inhibit the availability of land and limit the choice and variety of residential units that can be built.

Developers often find city codes and standards more restrictive than those of suburban jurisdictions, and the requirements typically lack the flexibility needed to address site-specific problems. While some practitioners can point to specific laws that raise their costs, the problem is usually that "most current zoning ordinances and development regulations have a strong suburban bias that would prohibit many favorite downtown and in-town neighborhoods from being built today. Usually, no single regulation is at fault; it is the sum total of all of the ordinances and regulations together."[6] Moreover, fees for building permits and utility connections tend to be high in urban neighborhoods.

Depending on the location and characteristics of the individual project, a number of environ-

## Citizen Participation

Improvements in the public planning process can enhance the political climate for infill development.

Involving citizens in the challenge of developing infill housing goes well beyond the traditional approaches to planning processes. Cities that have achieved the greatest success have begun with broad and inclusive efforts to create clear visions for their future. Rather than reacting to specific projects, they have endeavored to devise plans to implement their visions and have revised their approaches to citizen participation to encourage long-term collaboration among residents, businesspeople, and interest groups.

These efforts are ambitious. More than 4,000 citizens contributed to the Livable Region Strategy in Vancouver, British Columbia, Canada. In workshops, conferences, meetings, and questionnaires, they answered broad questions such as "Do people want to live at higher densities in order to preserve open space?" or "Would people be willing to walk or take transit to preserve air quality?" The conclusions forged a consensus for housing the region's next million residents in medium- and higher-density residential areas, rather than in low-density sprawl. Plans call for concentrating density in mixed-use centers, on obsolete industrial land, and in underused commercial areas.

The city of Pasadena, California, challenged citizens of a highly polarized community to Imagine a Greater City. After the participation of more than 3,200 residents and businesspeople, a new general plan was approved unanimously by both the planning commission and the city council and ratified by voters in the November 1992 election. Based on targeting infill development in transit corridors and around future light-rail stations, it anticipates making Pasadena "a city where people can circulate without cars."

Agreeing on a broad vision for infill development in a community helps build the foundation for efforts aimed at specific districts and sites. The next step is translating the broad vision for community revitalization into plans that target particular districts or sites for infill development. The city of San Jose, California, for example, has prepared a number of specific plans to implement its general plan's goal of intensification of housing along transit corridors. One of the first of these plans was the Jackson-Taylor Residential Strategy, intended for an area four blocks from a light-rail station and one mile from the

mental regulations can affect infill housing developments. The list of potentially applicable laws is long and includes, for example, the National Environmental Policy Act (NEPA), Clean Air Act, Clean Water Act, Safe Drinking Water Act, Noise Control Act, Endangered Species Act, Toxic Substances Control Act, Resources Conservation and Recovery Act, and Comprehensive Environmental Response, Compensation, and Liability Act (CERCLA).

CERCLA, in particular, affects redevelopment of vacant city land. The law was passed in 1980 to identify and prioritize sites contaminated with hazardous wastes and to assign legal responsibility for their contamination and cleaning. It also created a Superfund to help pay cleanup costs. CERCLA has been criticized for holding property purchasers, lenders, and others responsible— and legally liable—for site cleanup regardless of whether they were responsible for the environmental damage. It is also denigrated for imposing high cleanup standards that are costly and sometimes unrelated to a site's intended reuse, and for costing taxpayers a great deal while accomplishing only a small percentage of the needed cleanup. Several states have passed similar laws, resulting in confusion regarding which level of government and which standard applies, and which process must be followed.

Approximately 1,200 locations throughout the country have been designated as Superfund sites, and an estimated 400,000 or more as "brownfield" sites. Most of the sites that are candidates for reuse are the moderately contaminated brownfield sites, rather than the severely contaminated ones under Superfund. The precise magnitude of the brownfield problem is not known, though it is certainly significant. Virtually every community in the country contains abandoned or underused urban industrial land, often in prime locations.

Because of the environmental problems and the general physical and economic deterioration downtown. It dictates a transition for the old industrial warehouse district, full of vacant and abandoned buildings, into a walkable mixed-use neighborhood containing residences, offices, ground-floor retail, continuing industrial uses, and a daycare center.

Another example is Oakland, California, where the city, the Bay Area Rapid Transit District (BART), the community of Fruitvale, and the Spanish-Speaking Unity Council are all collaborating on a transit village plan for the Fruitvale BART station, encouraging both new development and the renovation of existing commercial businesses. The plan calls for a mix of homes, shops, and community-serving facilities, including a cultural center.

In pursuing new patterns of development, cities are beginning to use different approaches from the all-too-adversarial format of public decision making. Mayor Dan Kemmis of Missoula, Montana, writes of his experiences in his book, *Community and the Politics of Place,* that public hearings are the places in our society where no one listens. Many cities now use workshops, seminars, charrettes, and other informal, interactive settings to encourage dialogue, consensus, and give-and-take. Through these collaborative efforts, local governments can help educate the public about the connections between developments near them and the community costs and benefits of different patterns of development.

There are many new tools to help involve citizens in decisions about the future of their communities. Some cities are using the power of visual images, which are easy for non-planners and nonarchitects to work with. Architect Anton Nelessen, who teaches at Rutgers University, has pioneered using both slides of images within their communities and small building blocks to assist citizens in making choices about the kind of city they prefer. The Florida firm of Dover/Kohl makes imaginative use of computer simulations, while other companies put GIS technology to work. The Berkeley-based firm of Moore Iacofano Goltsman has designed simulation games in which citizens can work as teams on land use and transportation decisions.

*Sources:* Rick Cole, Nancy Bragado, Judy Corbett, and Sharon Sprowls; Local Government Commission; city of Sacramento, California.

experienced by older industrial areas in recent decades, it is a challenge to attract redevelopment to abandoned urban industrial sites. Cleanup costs may exceed the value of the site's most appropriate use, and investors are reluctant to expose themselves to the risk of potential liability. Consequently, the successful redevelopment of an individual site is unlikely without large-scale improvements to make the area more attractive to other types of investment.[7]

In addition, rehabilitation projects that involve historic buildings or that are located in historic districts must comply with the Secretary of the Interior's standards for rehabilitation. While these structures often present exciting development opportunities, compliance with historic preservation requirements imposes additional review requirements that add to the project's development time, expertise requirements, and development cost. The completed development may be well worth the extra effort; however, the developer must anticipate the requirements in advance to make an informed cost/benefit judgment on project feasibility.

Redevelopment of older buildings may require control or remediation of asbestos or lead-based paint hazards, which can also substantially increase development costs.

The various environmental laws affect where development can occur, what the development process will involve, what it will cost, how long it will take, and the ongoing costs to operate the development. Though advocates of individual regulations may rightly point out that a particular requirement imposes only modest compliance costs, the cumulative impact of all the applicable laws on an individual project can be substantial. Therefore, developers must carefully research potential environmental requirements before committing to a site or a project.

Government fragmentation contributes to the cost and complexity of development: city depart-

Sixty-four acres of the Randolph Neighborhood in Richmond, Virginia, cleared through urban renewal, have been reborn with historic and traditional amenities —front porches, front- and back-yards, brick facades, parks, and tree-lined streets that have enabled the newly built homes to blend in with the older, intact portions of the neighborhood.

ments pursuing different objectives may impose requirements that are difficult to meet simultaneously. Government fragmentation also can make land acquisition and development planning more difficult: much of the publicly owned, developable land in infill locations is owned by agencies or authorities that have acquired it in the course of pursuing various objectives and that have no well-considered plans for its development or disposal.

## Project Concept

Infill properties are often vacant because of some problem or obstacle to development, and "the real questions for the developer today are why would anyone want to live on the site now, who are the potential customers, what do they want, what can they afford, and which needs and wants can be satisfied on the property."[8]

With infill development, the answers to these questions are not obvious. Every project is different, and opportunities are often not readily apparent from a simple review of the numbers. A developer's familiar project model might not be the best fit for such environments. Developers need the magic combination of entrepreneurial skill, experience, local knowledge, imagination, and access to financing to create project concepts with the best market potential at the lowest cost and risk. And, according to Barry Humphries,

president of Renaissance Group of Columbus, Ohio, infill developers also need patience, good political instincts, and a willingness to work with diverse neighborhood interests.

For any given site, the developer might want to consider a broad range of uses and, in particular, innovative development options. Especially in weak markets, mixed-use projects can be a means of balancing risks by targeting different markets on the same site. Single-use developments are generally more risky, and single-use infill projects should as a rule be small. Larger single-use projects should be phased to minimize risk and to enable the developer to perfect the product as it develops.

## Design

Design of infill projects begins with an understanding of the physical, social, and economic conditions of the surrounding area. Unlike new subdivisions that sprout on suburban "greenfields," infill development occurs within an established historical and architectural context. Design of infill developments should be sensitive to the scale and texture of the surrounding neighborhood, though "contextual history manifested in architectural character and detail can wrap a new development whose density exceeds surrounding land uses in a friendly and comfortable face."[9]

At the same time, the project's design should strive to form for it a distinct identity, one that will give the development visibility and a positive image in the neighborhood.

Project design must be based on an understanding of the needs and preferences of the project's target market, and of what the competition is offering to that market. Especially in infill locations, it is important that project designers focus on the project's objectives rather than on preconceived ideas or conformance with prescribed standards.

And in these often-difficult development environments, project design must be cost-effective if the resulting housing is to be affordable to its intended market.

According to Elizabeth Moule of Moule & Polyzoides Architects of Los Angeles, design of city neighborhoods in general and of infill projects in particular must begin with an analysis of and respect for the existing environment, including understanding the neighborhood fabric and how housing is configured within it, and identifying and locating public buildings, nodes of activity, and the best streets. Urban neighborhoods should contain a mix of uses, pedestrian-friendly architecture (no blank walls), an orientation toward humans rather than automobiles, and a population diverse in ages and incomes. Infill development should be located within a five-minute walk of main streets and focal areas, such as parks, that give the neighborhood a sense of identity. Buildings should shape the street, and higher densities be encouraged and made more acceptable through fanciful architecture and a deemphasis on the automobile in the design of streets and parking. Civic buildings "should be the gems of our cities, rather than embarrassments."

One approach to gaining an understanding of the neighborhood's context is for the developer to inventory the neighborhood's characteristic design elements or, in other words, to "search for the 'soul of the place'" [10] through sketches, drawings, and old photos. Infill developments should

## Patching and Stitching: Design Principles for Residential Infill Development

The following design principles are based on longtime experience with and research on the historic patterns of streets and houses, and on sensitive public participation processes:

- *Involve existing residents.* Through focus groups and public meetings, determine residents' concerns and aspirations. They are the experts on their neighborhoods.
- *Study the context.* The historic inheritance of the housing and streets of the neighborhood and adjacent neighborhoods will be the keys to design.
- *Remember that the street is the focus.* Houses with porches should face the street with uniform setbacks, typically 20 to 25 feet. Garages should not face the street. Rear alleys should be considered for access to garages, trash collection, and utilities.
- *Provide links.* The urban neighborhood is part of the larger city. Ensure that streets connect to other neighborhoods and to city amenities and that public transit is available.
- *Combine infill with restoration.* The most successful projects artfully combine new infill housing with sensitive restoration of existing housing.
- *Provide a variety of housing.* A mix of single-family houses, townhouses, and apartments will furnish choices within a mixed-income neighborhood and housing for residents of all ages.
- *Develop a pattern book.* Architectural pattern books for the construction of facades and porches are useful in ensuring that builders conform to the design guidelines.
- *Construct or enhance amenities.* Streets should be lined with trees. Parks and recreation centers become gathering places for community life. Neighborhood retail shops and services should be found within walking distance of housing.

*Source:* Donald Carter, managing principal, Urban Design Associates, a Pittsburgh-based architectural and urban design firm.

Middle Towne Arch in Norfolk, Virginia, occupies a former public housing site located between Norfolk State University and industrial uses in what was considered "the wrong part of town." Architects from the firm of Urban Design Associates (UDA) prepared a master plan based on the city's prestigious and historic Ghent neighborhood and on design guidelines that reflect the nearby Williamsburg Historic District. By closely following these guidelines, the site's seven developers have produced an architecturally consistent, well-proportioned and -detailed neighborhood.

strive to establish a strong concept and vision, to focus the community, to maximize privacy and security, and to incorporate the residents' inevitable use of automobiles. While the project's colors should also respect the existing context, one observer recommends that developers use a variety of colors and intensities to avoid the look of a new project. Open space, public and private, is very important and, if sufficient, will make higher-density housing possible.

Parking is frequently an issue. In most, though not all, city housing markets, how the developer or sponsor proposes to handle parking for residents and visitors is an important factor that affects a project's demand potential. The number of proposed off-street parking spaces in relation to the number of housing units that will be provided must comply with the zoning and must be sufficient to satisfy the intended target market for the proposed housing units.

Security is often a major concern in inner-city areas, and infill housing developments can promote security through design.[11] In the Westminster Place development in St. Louis, the safety issue has been addressed by incorporating strategic security features such as alarm systems in each unit, parking close to unit entrances, and unit configurations that allow surveillance of the parking areas from residents' kitchens. The main entryways in the rental apartment buildings are locked, eliminating the potential hazard of open stairwells. The street system was designed to control circulation through the development: to keep outside people from penetrating the area, major traffic arteries were located along the perimeters of buildings, and traffic through the development was confined to a few interior streets. And following the St. Louis tradition of private neighborhood streets, some streets at Westminster were gated to allow better traffic monitoring. Plantings and taste-

ful fencing were also used to connect buildings so that the project is not a sieve through which people can walk.[12]

Affordability is another concern that can be addressed through design. Particularly where affordability is an issue, manufactured houses hold some promise for enabling developers to produce efficient, attractive infill housing that will serve many markets well. To promote the use of manufactured houses in infill locations, the Manufactured Housing Institute (MHI) recently began a two-year demonstration project known as the Urban Design Project as part of its participation in President Clinton's National Homeownership Partnership. Under the leadership of Susan Maxman of Susan Maxman Architects, Philadelphia, MHI and its member manufacturers will work with local teams in six U.S. cities[13] to create and install architecturally appropriate manufactured houses in infill locations with a shortage of decent affordable housing. The resulting design prototypes are intended to help developers, lenders, local governments, funders, and service agencies involved in housing provision to understand the potential for the use of manufactured houses to meet the need for affordable, architecturally compatible housing. The demonstration will also help the traditionally rural manufactured housing industry to reach a better understanding of how housing is delivered in urban environments.

Developer Paul Wang of Berkeley, California, has successfully used manufactured houses to fill in scattered vacant lots in the Elmhurst neighborhood of Oakland, California. The homes are compatible in size and scale with existing houses in the community and include site-built garages, private patios, and false fronts that make the homes look like they have conventionally constructed pitched roofs. The manufactured homes are offered at prices that are approximately half the median price of a typical newly constructed house in the vicinity.

Modular houses can also be used to provide affordable housing on infill sites. In the Trinity Court development, for instance, the developer used modular construction to develop 30 two- and three-bedroom townhouses for first-time buyers on an infill site in a transitional neighborhood. The modular components were built in a factory and assembled and finished on the site. While modular units made the houses affordable, the developer added roof gables, bay windows, doorways with cornices, shutters, and landscaping to add variety and individualism.

Properly designed manufactured homes can be a good choice for urban infill sites. Laurel Courts, a fee-simple community of single- and multisection manufactured homes in Oakland, California, was built at a density of 17.5 units per acre using zero-lot-line placements.

## Manufactured Homes for Infill Development

Manufactured homes—formerly called mobile homes—are built in a factory and meet the preemptive standards of the U.S. Department of Housing and Urban Development (HUD) performance code. Each house has a permanent chassis on which it is transported to a site that the homeowner owns or rents. During installation, two or more sections of the home may be joined; the home is then enhanced through site-built additions like porches or garages and through landscaping.

Manufactured houses have several advantages over stick-built houses. First, they cost less to produce and are therefore more affordable for buyers. The production process is fast, flexible, and cost-efficient. Construction and financing costs are lower. The home can be installed on site and sealed within an eight-hour period, with minimum vulnerability to vandalism. Because the homes are built in a factory, they can

be modified to make them compatible with existing development or customized to fit a particular market niche. Moreover, they can be manufactured locally by local residents, thereby generating jobs for inner-city inhabitants.

Manufactured houses can be sited successfully on infill parcels if they can be made architecturally compatible with existing housing—for example, in roof pitch, overhangs, exterior finishes, and architectural style—without significantly changing the way a manufacturer builds. Doing so requires cooperation among the manufacturer, the local developer, and a professional architect. Homes intended for infill lots must also be responsive to market demands, affordable, and acceptable to city and state officials.

For manufactured houses to be usable in infill development, local ordinances must allow HUD-code homes within the jurisdiction. To help meet the

burgeoning demand for affordable houses, California in 1980 passed a law allowing the siting of HUD-code homes on any lot except where existing covenants, conditions, and restrictions specifically exclude them, so long as they are architecturally compatible with existing houses. As a result, much of the innovative experience with the use of manufactured homes has been gained in California.

In the Old Town area of San Pablo, California, for example, a for-profit developer successfully used manufactured homes to replace more than 50 deteriorated houses on infill lots. On one block, the developer mixed two-story, site-built houses with manufactured homes to demonstrate their compatibility in design.

*Source:* From a ULI symposium, "Developing Infill Housing," held in Milwaukee, September 14–15, 1995.

# Mount Pleasant Homes, Cleveland, Ohio

Fifty new single-family houses were built on scattered sites in the Mount Pleasant and Central neighborhoods of Cleveland.

As the Mount Pleasant Homes development demonstrates, infill housing can be developed successfully on scattered sites.

In Cleveland, The Zaremba Group, Inc.—in partnership with the nonprofit, community-based Mount Pleasant Now Development Corporation and Lutheran Housing Corporation—developed 50 new single-family houses in the scattered-site development known as Mount Pleasant Homes. The project represents the first newly constructed home development to be offered on a lease-purchase basis in Cleveland.

The project, situated in the Mount Pleasant and Central neighborhoods of Cleveland, was created to redevelop individual vacant lots acquired by the city through tax foreclosure. The sites had become cluttered with garbage and other debris and were a blight on the neighborhood.

The three- and four-bedroom houses, which average 1,200 to 1,300 square feet, have color-coordinated exteriors, full basements, garages, and electronic security systems. Because the market includes a large number of single mothers with children, houses are sited to ensure privacy and play areas for children.

Financing for the $4.2 million Mount Pleasant Homes development has included $3.4 million in equity from the National Equity Fund (the nation's largest syndicator of federal low-income housing tax credits); a $400,000 loan from the city's 1992 Housing Trust Fund; a $2 million bridge loan from the state of Ohio; and 15-year tax abatements from the city of Cleveland. Huntington Bank is providing a loan of $3.5 million for construction and a $1.25 million permanent loan. Though households earning up to 60 percent of the median area income are eligible to participate, the city's subsidy enables rents to be set within the reach of families earning incomes of 30 percent of the area median.

Occupants rent their houses for the tax credit compliance period, after which time a qualified tenant may buy the house for the amount of the remaining debt. Tenants receive home-ownership counseling from Mount Pleasant Now Development Corporation.

Mount Pleasant Now Development Corporation is active in other neighborhood improvement and development activities, including programs to tutor youths, rehabilitate housing, and eliminate drugs, and the development of a new planned-unit community.

Since completion of the Mount Pleasant Homes development in 1994, The Zaremba Group has built and leased a similar 50-unit project with the same partners. In addition, the firm has developed, with similar groups, 200 other scattered-site houses for lease-purchase by low-income families in other inner-city sections of Cleveland.

# Hollywood El Centro, Los Angeles, California

Hollywood El Centro is a good example of how a well-designed, well-managed, adaptive use residential development can help transform a distressed low-income neighborhood.

Hollywood El Centro is an award-winning, 87-unit residential development for low-income households standing on a 1.72-acre site adjacent to the Hollywood Community Hospital. The developer, Thomas Safran & Associates (TSA), rehabilitated 15 one- and two-story buildings on ten contiguous lots and created a stable redeveloped commu-

Hollywood El Centro is shown before and after rehabilitation.

nity within a marginal neighborhood of Hollywood south of Sunset Boulevard. The project, begun in 1993, was completed in 1996.

## Background

At the time of purchase, the 15 existing buildings were 60 percent occupied by very-low-income persons but were in poor physical condition. The buildings were the headquarters of the TMC 13th Street Gang and had become a haven for drug and prostitution activities in the neighborhood. Young teenagers with guns and pagers moved freely about the buildings during the evenings. Police hesitated to enter the buildings unless backed up by several squad cars; one of the buildings contained a crack house where 16 people occupied a single unit, sleeping on wall-to-wall mattresses. Caches of stolen Uzis and shotguns were found hidden in the garages of the development.

Gradually, the community was taken back from the gangs. The first stage was to relocate the individuals who were causing these problems, a process that took a year and a half. The community supported the relocation efforts and the police efforts to oust gang activities. The developer erected security fences temporarily among the buildings to keep the gangs out, and when the gangs used car jacks to open up the bars of the fences, the developer covered the bars in black roofing tar. Lights were added behind bulletproof screens, and eventually the gang members could no longer conduct their activities in comfort.

Today, the development combines small and larger units at a density of 50 units to the acre. The buildings, built between 1920 and 1930, vary in architectural style. Some are architecturally or historically significant. All buildings now meet or exceed code requirements.

## Design

To integrate the buildings physically, off-white stucco and deep-green trim were used as continuing design elements. The developer linked the buildings with a light security mesh fence set back from the faces of the structures and covered with landscaping. The project perimeter is marked by a three-foot planter wall that separates it from the sidewalk, and its gated entrances feature a computerized entry system for visitors.

To fashion an entryway to the development that would also serve as community space, the developer constructed new interior space in what had been a driveway and built two ground-floor units that now stand between two two-story buildings on the southern boundary of the site. In addition to the community room, this area also includes a recreation room, computer training center, kitchen, central mail facility, manager's office, bathrooms, and central laundry.

Rear yards of the buildings were graded and combined to form an interior courtyard with parking for 18 cars (only 13 had been required by the previous building permits). The courtyard also contains outdoor community facilities such as a half-size basketball court that

doubles as a place to ride bicycles, and an outdoor community barbecue and picnic ground. All utilities were moved underground, and the development has been heavily landscaped to provide privacy and views.

On the eastern portion of the site, part of one building was demolished to clear a wider space for automobiles to enter the central courtyard. As there was not enough space for adequate resident parking on site, the developer sought a residents' parking district designation in the neighborhood that would restrict street parking to residents during the evening hours.

## Financing

The project cost nearly $12 million to complete. The developer committed family equity to hold the property while assembling the financing and wresting control of the buildings from the street gangs. TSA purchased the property with a portion of a $4 million loan from the Community Redevelopment Agency (CRA), through a five-year, interest-only land loan from the previous owner of the property. The developer received $5 million in federal low-income housing tax credits (LIHTCs) for the project and supplemented these with a $730,000 Affordable Housing Program (AHP) grant from the Federal Home Loan Bank of San Francisco.

Home Savings of America provided a construction/permanent rollover loan secured by the tax credits. And a corporate investor, Mission First (now Edison Capital) purchased the tax credits, providing equity to the development, and was in-

## Summary of Project Financing

| | |
|---|---:|
| Permanent Loan (Home Savings of America) ($3.6 million advanced by Home Savings during construction; the difference paid off with additional equity funds from Mission/Edison Capital) | $2,120,000 |
| AHP Grant (FHLBB of San Francisco) | 730,638 |
| Residual Receipts (soft second from the CRA of the city of Los Angeles) | 4,011,591 |
| Equity (for the federal LIHTCs) | |
|     Mission First Financial (now known as Edison Capital) | 5,029,098 |
|     Thomas Safran & Associates (TSA) | 85,880 |
| Total | $11,977,207 |

strumental in advancing funds when necessary to ensure the timely completion of the project. (See the summary of the project financing.)

The project also received 87 HUD Section 8 certificates for the development, which serves households at or below 50 percent of the area median income. Twenty percent of the units have been set aside for special-needs families (mainly, formerly homeless single parents with children). The development will be income-restricted for at least 55 years.

Initially, about 41 families were retained in the development. Keeping these families called for organizing the project construction into two phases and moving the families between the residential units as development proceeded. Twenty-three of these families were eventually relocated, including 12 families who bought homes with the relocation funds; 18 of the initial 41 families remained with Hollywood El Centro at project completion.

Because of its large size and visibility, the development has

had a profound effect on the surrounding neighborhood. For example, buildings across the street have been rehabilitated into apartments that lease for as much as $1,200 per month. Through Hollywood El Centro, previously crime-ridden, ramshackle buildings have been reborn as components of a beautiful, landscaped development that relates harmoniously to the street and to its neighbors and provides decent, safe, and sanitary housing for 87 very-low-income families.

*Source:* Thomas Safran & Associates.

# Mercy Family Plaza, San Francisco, California

Development of Mercy Family Plaza in San Francisco preserved architectural elements like the smokestack and the striking arched openings of the Power House building, and gave the buildings a new, lightened color scheme.

The award-winning Mercy Family Plaza shows how preservation of historic buildings can make possible the development of distinctive, neighborhood-enhancing affordable housing.

Combining the goals of historic preservation and affordable housing, buildings of the Southern Pacific/ Harkness Hospital complex—San Francisco's oldest hospital complex—have been reincarnated as 36 units of low-income fam-

ily housing. Achieving this harmonious result was anything but easy: the pre-1930 brick buildings required seismic strengthening, and the project had to meet the stringent historic rehabilitation standards set by the Secretary of the Interior. At the same time, a tight budget had to be met, and a financing package had to be assembled that would make the project financially feasible without federal assistance.

The Mercy Family Plaza buildings consist of the former

Huntington Social Hall, Nurses' Annex, Power House, and utility building/toolshed. The Nurses' Annex, at four stories the largest of the four buildings, is connected to the former main hospital building by a pedestrian bridge.

The four-story, rectangular Nurses' Annex was reconfigured by project architects Sandy & Babcock, Inc., to accommodate 24 of the project's 36 residential units, and the bridge was converted into an airy laundry room. The Power House, a tall, one-story building with arched 12-foot-high windows and an 80-foot-tall chimney, was converted into eight two-story units by the introduction of a partial second floor.

The Social Hall, a two-story structure, was converted into four large apartments around the original terrazzo-and-tile entry stair. The fourth building, a small, one-story utility building adjacent to the Nurses' Annex, was converted for use as a recreation room with kitchenette, and its roof was finished as a terrace and roof garden.

## The Site

Mercy Family Plaza is part of the one-square-block site formerly occupied by the Southern Pacific/Harkness Hospital complex. The site lies one block from the panhandle of Golden Gate Park, in a neighborhood of typical San Francisco Victorian-era townhouses. The neighborhood is mixed in income and ethnicity. Across the street is a bed-and-breakfast guesthouse in a restored Victorian building. Next to the site on a second side is a meditation center in a similarly restored townhouse.

The hospital buildings on the site, designed on a monumental scale in the Neoclassical style, were built between 1907 and 1930. Two had been renovated for other uses during the 1960s but were later vacated. The hospital closed its doors in 1973, and the site sat vacant until it was acquired in 1982 by Mercy Services Corporation, a nonprofit subsidiary of the Sisters of Mercy, the nation's largest Catholic order.

The main high-rise hospital building at the front of the site, dubbed Mercy Terrace, was renovated in 1983 as a 158-unit seniors' housing project under the HUD Section 8 program. The four outbuildings, to the rear of the site, remained vacant and boarded up until construction of Mercy Family Plaza in 1990.

## Development Process

In the late 1980s, Mercy Family Housing California (MFHC, now known as Mercy Charities Housing) agreed to develop housing on the rear portion of the hospital site. As sponsor and general partner of the project, MFHC asked the Ibex Group, a development partnership, to produce a turnkey project for low-income families.

The feasibility of preserving the historic hospital buildings was predicated on the project's being able to obtain and sell both low-income housing tax credits and historic rehabilitation investment tax credits. Use of the rehabilitation tax credits meant that the new use had to be put in service within two years and that the rehab had to be certified as complying with the *Secretary's Standards* (the Secretary of the Interior's standards for historic rehabilitation projects). This included maintaining and renovating, or replacing exactly, all "character-defining elements" of the original construction.

In planning the development, John Stewart of Ibex worked closely with neighborhood residents, the Landmarks Preserva-

tion Advisory Board, the State Historic Preservation Officer, and the National Park Service to respond to their concerns and to define the key areas of historic significance. Because these issues were resolved during project planning, the review process was comparatively swift and uncomplicated.

## Design and Construction

Due to previous remodelings, abandonment, vandalism, and fire, the interiors of the buildings had been completely destroyed. Therefore, the developers almost entirely gutted the interiors of the four hospital buildings to make way for the residential units, though some original features, such as the entry hall and elevator of the Social Hall, were retained. Concrete seismic "shear walls" were installed inside the original brick exterior walls, and a new floor was inserted into the high-ceilinged Power House to create a two-story building. New mechanical, electrical, and plumbing systems were installed.

Building exteriors were preserved intact, with the exception of new unit entry doors, which were built into some of the oversized windows, and repainting of the brick facades. A second task was to seismically reinforce the Power House's smokestack, which was saved because it was a "character-defining element."

Some of the most interesting interior detailing at Mercy Family Plaza resulted from compliance with historic preservation requirements. At the Power House, in order to preserve the appearance of the building, with its monumental windows, and to enable light emanating from the windows to illuminate both floors, the second-story floors were recessed from the windows. The city's building department, however, required access to the window head as a means of providing emergency egress from the second-floor sleeping areas. The ingenious design solution was to craft a "drawbridge," a metal grate that normally functions as a guardrail at the slab edge but flips down in an emergency to connect to the egress window.

A two-level parking structure was built in place of the existing 36-car parking lot at the west end of the site that was serving Mercy Terrace, the seniors' housing development. The new 73-space structure allows the seniors to continue to park on the grade level and enter through their own vehicle gate, while the Mercy Family Plaza residents park on the upper deck and enter by a gate at that level.

# Mercy Family Plaza Project Data

## Land Use Information[1]

Site Area: 1 acre
Total Dwelling Units: 36
Gross Density: 36 units per acre
Off-Street Parking Spaces: 44[2]

## Land Use Plan

|  | Acres | Percent of Site |
|---|---|---|
| Buildings | 0.42 | 42 |
| Roads/Paved Areas | 0.13 | 13 |
| Common Open Space (including recreation) | 0.07 | 7 |
| Parking Structure | 0.38 | 38 |
| Total | 1.00 | 100 |

## Financing Information

Permanent and Bridge Financing Sources

| | |
|---|---|
| SAMCO (permanent loan) | $3,386,000 |
| State of California grant | 321,000 |
| San Francisco Affordable Housing Fund | 200,000 |
| Markborough California Properties in-lieu fee | 677,000 |
| Low-Income Housing Foundation and McAuley Foundation loans | 360,000 |
| Long-term, below-market purchase money note from seller | 500,000 |
| Total | $5,444,000 |

Other Financing Sources[3]

| | |
|---|---|
| Union Bank (construction loan) | $3,300,000 |
| Low-income housing tax credits and historic rehabilitation investment tax credits[3] | $4,430,000 |

## Development Cost Information

| | |
|---|---|
| Site Acquisition Cost | $500,000 |
| Site Improvement Costs | |
|   Sitework | $177,000 |
|   Landscaping | 71,000 |
|   Total | $248,000 |
| Construction Costs | |
|   Building | $2,623,705 |
|   Seismic bracing | 447,158 |
|   Asbestos removal | 90,275 |
|   Parking garage | 383,800 |
|   Personal property | 120,000 |
|   Total | $3,664,938 |
| Soft Costs | |
|   Architecture/engineering | $414,904 |
|   Developer fee | 682,441 |
|   Marketing | 17,941 |
|   Interest and financing fees | 455,357 |
|   Permits | 70,400 |
|   Other | 199,358 |
|   Total | $1,840,401 |
| Total Development Cost | $6,253,339 |

Total Development Cost per Unit: $173,000
Construction Cost per Square Foot: $187.50

1. The site for this project is part of a historic hospital complex that encompasses an entire city block. Any study of the project should keep these existing conditions in mind, as they affect the implications of considerations such as density and costs.

2. A new parking structure provides 38 new parking spaces above 35 existing parking spaces, with additional six spaces located on grade elsewhere on the site, for a total of 79. These areas provide parking for both projects, with 44 spaces allocated for Mercy Family Plaza.

3. Projected over a ten-year period.

*Source: Excerpted from ULI Project Reference File report, Volume 24, Number 20.*

The spaces between the residential buildings and the parking garage serve as pleasantly landscaped interior walkways, with ornamental lighting and benches. A tot lot and basketball court have also been provided. Between Mercy Terrace and Mercy Family Plaza is a blacktop emergency-vehicle lane, which does double duty as a venue for holiday parties, barbecues, and other joint activities. At the site's perimeter, the original decorative iron fence surrounding the hospital grounds has been maintained for security, and new gates with card readers have been installed.

## Financing

Ten separate financing sources were required, including the syndication of low-income housing tax credits and historic rehabilitation tax credits. Fannie Mae, as the sole limited partner in the project, purchased all of the available tax credits with a contribution of $4.4 million in equity payments spread over ten years. In addition, funding for the project included the following: a contribution from Markborough California Properties through the city of San Francisco's Office of Affordable Housing Production program; a grant from the city of San Francisco's Affordable Housing Fund; a grant from the state of California; construction financing from Union Bank; and permanent financing from the Savings Association Mortgage Company (SAMCO). The McAuley Foundation provided a below-market bridge loan, as did the Low-Income Housing Foundation. The seller, who leased the property to Mercy Charities Housing for 99 years with a proviso that it be used for affordable housing, provided a below-market purchase money note.

The developer of Mercy Family Plaza, the Ibex Group, will receive a development fee and syndication fee paid out over the first eight years of the project.

## Marketing/ Management

Care was taken to attract a multicultural mix of tenants for Mercy Family Plaza through an outreach program to solicit tenants from nearby neighborhoods and congregations of all faiths. Preference in selection was given to families and to residents of San Francisco.

The project was 100 percent leased before completion and has had a waiting list ever since. Unit turnover has been low, especially for the larger units; smaller apartments (studios and one-bedroom units) turn over more frequently because their rents are closer to market rents.

**Chapter Notes**

1. Nancy Bragado, Judy Corbett, and Sharon Sprowls, *Building Livable Communities: A Policymaker's Guide to Infill Development* (Washington, D.C.: Center for Livable Communities and Local Government Commission, 1995), pp. 6–7.

2. Professor Joe Gyourko, quoted in Doug Donsky, "Real Estate Has Key Role in Rebuilding U.S. Cities," *Commercial Property News* (December 1, 1992), p. 26.

3. William H. Kreager, "Developing Infill Housing," *Land Development* (Winter 1996), p. 10.

4. Kreager, "Developing Infill Housing," p. 11.

5. Rick Cole, Nancy Bragado, Judy Corbett, and Sharon Sprowls, "Building Livable Communities: New Strategies for Promoting Infill Development," *Urban Land* (September 1996).

6. Bragado, Corbett, and Sprowls, *Building Livable Communities*, p. 5.

7. Excerpted from Diane R. Suchman, *Cityscape*, Volume 2, Number 3 (Washington, D.C.: U.S. Department of Housing and Urban Development, Office of Policy Development and Research, September 1996).

8. Kreager, "Developing Infill Housing," p. 9.

9. Ibid., p. 11.

10. Ibid.

11. For more information on defensible design, see Oscar Newman, *Creating Defensible Space* (Washington, D.C.: U.S. Department of Housing and Urban Development, Office of Policy Development and Research, April 1996).

12. From a *ULI Project Reference File* report written by Terry Lassar, to be published online in January 1998.

13. Cities selected to participate in the demonstration are Milwaukee; Denver; Louisville; Birmingham, Alabama; Washington, D.C.; and Wilkinsburg, Pennsylvania.

# CHAPTER 4

# Mixed-Income Housing

Mixed-income housing has increasingly attracted attention from developers and public officials who are interested in creating more diverse city neighborhoods and expanding housing opportunities for low- and moderate-income families. Development of mixed-income communities generates many benefits to project residents and to the larger community but involves an additional array of development considerations.

Living in a mixed-income environment, lower-income families enjoy a better, more secure physical environment than in an entirely low-income neighborhood and a more beneficial social milieu that includes positive, economically independent role models. When asked why he entered the mixed-income housing business, Joseph Corcoran, chairman of Corcoran Jennison Companies in Boston, has commented that he began to develop government-assisted housing in 1971 but soon felt "there had to be a better way to house the poor, in a better environment—the government should not be building ghettos."

Numerous studies have confirmed Corcoran's twofold hunch: that concentrating poor people in poor neighborhoods perpetuates social and economic problems, and that moving to a more diverse environment encourages and enables families to improve their employment, earnings, and educational achievement. Mixed-income housing not only constitutes a better environment for low-income families, but also it provides all residents with the security of knowing that they can remain in place if their circumstances change. Low-income tenants can move into market-rate units in the same development if they earn more

money; likewise, market-rate tenants whose incomes decline may not need to move out if their incomes fall within the qualifying range for below-market units.

Perhaps the most compelling reason to build or encourage mixed-income housing is that it is the most effective way to revitalize declining areas. In urban areas, mixed-income housing can contribute to neighborhood revitalization efforts by bringing in residents with more buying power to support local businesses. At the same time, it can help meet the needs of a diverse group of urban workers who prefer to live in the city. Richard Baron of McCormack Baron & Associates in St. Louis comments that in trying to rebuild neighborhoods, he takes a long-term view, and large concentrations of poor residents just will not work over the long term: "To create the economics necessary for neighborhood revitalization, you have to bring in higher-income people."

Mixed-income housing is defined here as housing developments that include both subsidized and market-rate units. The discussion in this chapter does not refer to projects that encourage a mix of lower-income households among units that are all subsidized. Nor does it include developments produced through inclusionary zoning programs. (Inclusionary zoning programs typically require developers of new housing developments that contain more than a certain number of units to include a fixed percentage of units that are affordable to moderate-income households. In exchange for fulfilling this requirement, the developer usually is granted

Ellen Wilson
Dwellings,
Washington,
D.C., before
transformation to
a mixed-income
development.

a density bonus, which is intended to enable the developer to generate sufficient additional profit to cover the cost of providing the lower-cost units. Often, the moderately priced homes produced through inclusionary housing programs are physically separate from and smaller than other units in the development.)

Like other types of infill housing development, mixed-income projects take many forms. A mixed-income development can offer rentals, for-sale housing, or a combination. Units can be single-family houses, townhouses, or apartments. The development can involve rehabilitation, new construction, or both. Additional uses, such as retail or recreational space, may or may not be included. Projects can be developed by private for-profit developers, nonprofit developers, public agencies, joint for-profit/nonprofit ventures, or public/private partnerships.

Individual developers tend to specialize in certain types of projects. For example, McCormack Baron & Associates typically initiates large-scale redevelopment within cities, on the fringe of the business district near concentrations of major employers and businesses. The Corcoran Jennison Companies creates mixed-income communities from failed public housing or publicly subsidized projects. The BRIDGE Housing Corporation, a nonprofit developer in the San Francisco area that often forms joint ventures with for-profit developers, builds mixed-income hous-

ing in higher-income suburbs as well as within urbanized areas.

As with other types of residential development, the specific market served will vary with the project. The targeting and income mix of any given project will vary, typically depending on the requirements attached to one or more of the funding sources, the public policy goals of the local jurisdiction, and the particular expertise or interest of the developer.

## Market Considerations

According to Richard Ward of Development Strategies, Inc. (DSI), in St. Louis, successful development of mixed-income communities—like other types of infill housing development—depends upon a careful assessment of the market. DSI conducts many of the market studies for McCormack Baron's mixed-income developments, including direct attitudinal surveys. According to these surveys, "In most central-city locations, there are people with different lifestyles and incomes who are interested in the same housing product and who are willing to pay a range of prices for it." The people who choose to live in market-rate apartments in mixed-income developments "are typically not doctors and stockbrokers but teachers, nurses, and service sector workers who might otherwise be forced to move out of the city." Because downtown employees, particularly those working in hospitals and universities, are accustomed to being with a variety of people on a daily basis, they are more comfortable living among a diverse population.

Ward recounts that when DSI conducted a market research survey 25 years ago for the Ralston-Purina Company, DSI was astounded to learn that Ralston-Purina's employees would be interested in living in a nearby, deteriorated neighborhood if decent housing (like the proposed project) were available. The research was borne out by behavior after the fact: the project successfully attracted its intended market. Jon Wellhoefer, executive vice president of the Milwaukee Redevelopment Corporation, concurs, noting that downtown employers—particularly universities, hospitals, and insurance companies—employ thousands of people who would prefer to live within walking distance of their work. According to Wellhoefer, the challenge to developers is to find ways to meet this potential demand by responding to the workers' housing, neighborhood, and lifestyle needs. For example, single parents prefer their homes, daycare, and jobs to be near one another. Wellhoefer suggests that developers work with the personnel directors of large downtown employers to identify potential market niches and to pinpoint their needs.

As noted, the market served and the precise income mix will depend not only on the need or market demand but also on the requirements of the available subsidies. Thus, the income distribution varies widely among projects. Depending on the funders' requirements and the local median household income, income limits for below-market-rate units also will differ from project to project.

Some types of income distribution seem to work better than others. In Tent City, a 269-unit rental apartment complex in downtown Boston that also includes some ground-level retail and underground parking, 25 percent of the homes are for low-income households (earning 50 percent or less of the city median income), 50 percent are for moderate-income households (earning 50 to 120 percent of the city median income), and 25 percent are market-rate units. According to the nonprofit developer, Tent City Corporation, the 50 percent moderate-income tier makes the mixed-income aspect of the project work because no obvious gap separates lower-income residents from those paying the full market rate. (According to the developer, however, it is difficult to find subsidies that encourage this type of mix.)

## Development Process

The process for developing mixed-income housing essentially is the same as for other types of residential development. As illustrated, however, by the development of Quality Hill, a 25-block urban redevelopment project that has provided market-rate and affordable rental housing within a historic district in Kansas City, Missouri, mixed-income projects can involve complicated public/private partnerships. The cooperation and common commitment of public agencies, funders, and the developer are essential to meeting the challenges posed by these complex developments and to achieving the desired goals.

### Project Design

To attract market-rate buyers or renters, mixed-income housing projects must be "as nice as or nicer than competing developments." The development must incorporate the same careful attention to planning, community design, and architectural features that characterizes a well-designed market-rate community. According to Jim Wentling of James Wentling/Architects in Philadelphia, good design should include the use of historically compatible, regionally appropriate architecture wherever possible.

Most practitioners recommend that, in the design of a mixed-income development, it is important to integrate the subsidized units into the community fully so that no one knows who is living in a subsidized unit and who is paying market rates. There should be no distinction among the units, internal or external, other than perhaps the presence of amenities such as upgraded finishings, fireplaces, or views.

One of the more ambitious mixed-income projects is in El Cerrito, California, where the Ibex Group, in partnership with the city of El Cerrito, achieved a number of goals in developing "the mother of all hybrids," Del Norte Place, a mixed-use, mixed-income rental project located at a Bay Area Rapid Transit (BART) station. Designed to encourage more transit use, the project contains 135 residential units in four buildings, one of which is designated for senior citizens. The project also has 21,000 square feet of retail space.

As a general rule, however, in a mixed-income development, the developer—and the project's funders—must resist the temptation to complicate the project excessively by trying to accomplish too many different goals at once. For example, the inclusion of a retail component can make the financing more difficult, impose additional construction requirements, and make the project harder to lease.

## Size

Creating a critical mass of development activity, with adequate accessways, is especially important in inner-city revitalization activities that involve building mixed-income communities. If the development is located in a blighted inner-city area, the housing development that is proposed (or the housing development and adjacent revitalization activity) must be large enough to establish its own neighborhood, to show clearly that the area is changing, and to prove that revitalization activity is well enough along to preclude a return to the former, blighted conditions. Reaching a critical mass of development activity is especially important when inner-city, for-sale housing units are being proposed in a formerly blighted or deteriorated place because potential buyers are being asked to invest their own money in the neighborhood.

Even for rental housing, however, achieving sufficient critical mass to attract residents to an area requires the fashioning in a single project or several contiguous projects of an image of a revitalized community that is a safe, stable neighborhood. Whether the objective is to provide new opportunities for existing residents of the community, to attract new residents to the area, or both, the housing development that is proposed cannot achieve long-term success if it is a small, isolated project in an otherwise deteriorated district.

## Financing

As a general rule, mixed-income housing cannot be financed successfully through conventional financing models and funding sources. Instead, the financing typically will involve piecing together funds from a number of public and private sources. Thus, the financing for each project will be different and will depend on the nature of the project, the types and levels of funding sources available at the state and local levels, and the degree of local public commitment to the project's goals. (Public/private financing strategies are the subject of Chapter 5.)

## Marketing

Marketing strategies for mixed-income developments follow the same general pattern as those for all market-rate projects. But certain specific issues must be addressed in attracting market-rate

buyers or renters. For example, in for-sale projects, prospective market-rate buyers may be concerned that the subsidized units will be occupied by unemployed people; in fact, a minimum income typically is required to qualify for purchasing subsidized units. Buyers of market-rate units who may object to subsidizing the units of lower-income households need to be made aware of other offsets that make reduced prices or rents possible. The developer also will need to respond to concerns about the long-term value of the property, management practices, and tenant selection.[1]

Mixed-income housing attracts buyers or renters of market-rate units who like the location, the unit, and the community and who feel they are getting a good value. Tom Costello, vice president for management at McCormack Baron & Associates, observes, "Generally, we sell urban living and proximity to employment centers."

Some may be skeptical because of the neighborhood character or because they prefer to live in an economically segregated environment. According to Corcoran, "You will always lose about 15 percent of the market because some buyers don't want to live with low-income people. On the other hand, some people admire the concept and rent because of it." Others may find comfort in the knowledge that they can stay put if their incomes fall. For example, residents of market-rate units in projects designed for senior citizens may like the assurance that rent-assisted units will be available to them, when vacated, if their assets become depleted.

Recommended strategies for marketing mixed-income communities include attracting area residents by reaching out to the local community, and/or following the basic marketing principles of meeting with local brokers, preparing a high-quality brochure, using good signage, and advertising in the local media, especially at a project's opening. McCormack Baron & Associates observes that its best marketing strategy has been to target its outreach to firms in the community whose employees might be interested in living near their work.

As with any market-rate development, it is easier to sell market-rate units when demand is strong. But typically, the mixed-income aspect of the development does not slow project absorption. As the experiences of mixed-income developments throughout the country have shown, attractive mixed-income developments that offer market-responsive amenities, high-quality housing, good value, and a safe environment can compete for tenants with market-rate developments.

Yet some developers, like Thomas Safran of Los Angeles, prefer to develop projects with all low-income units because there is virtually no risk in rent-up. According to Safran, "If the market will support it, mixed-income housing is preferable for families as a means of creating a more stable neighborhood. Nevertheless, developments in which all units are below market rate are easier to rent because the demand is greater than the supply." The primary challenge in filling the subsidized units is tenant selection, as discussed in the next section of this chapter.

## Management

After quality, management is the most important ingredient of success in mixed-income developments. Management of mixed-income housing is similar in many respects to management of any housing development, but the inclusion of low-income families presents additional challenges. According to John Stewart, president of The John Stewart Companies of San Francisco, mixed-income housing imposes additional paperwork in the form of the income recertifications and waiting lists required by various housing programs and financing sources. These administrative costs, however, are "probably offset by the stability of the tenant population in below-market-rate units and the guaranteed rent payments from various rent subsidy programs."

Observes Corcoran, mixed-income developments "require more care and feeding than the average. We train our people and move them from one development to another. The procedures and philosophy are embedded in the company."

In the case of new construction, low-income tenant applicants can and should be carefully screened. Careful screening involves checking third-party references, verifying income, checking credit, checking police records, and visiting applicants at home—to make sure that the number of people in the household is the same as that indicated on the application, to verify the current address, to note housekeeping standards, and to observe any obvious social problems. Though essential, these checks can prove time-consuming.

According to Tom Costello, McCormack Baron & Associates typically follows the same screening procedure for all tenants, market-rate and low-income. "Although this can get ticklish at times, the market-rate tenants usually like the idea when they think about it. They know we are serious and really do care who comes into the community."

Nevertheless, when an existing low-income project is converted into a mixed-income community, the project must accept the existing tenants—though they are required to sign a new lease. Many existing residents can be expected to have problems and will need help with, for example, housekeeping and parenting skills, finding a job, or dealing with substance abuse. Corcoran observes that his firm has had to evict perhaps 10 percent of a project's original residents for failure to comply with lease requirements.

To minimize these kinds of problems, the Corcoran Jennison Companies employs an outside firm, Housing Opportunities Unlimited (HOU), to

The mixed-income Centennial Place has replaced the former Techwood and Clark Howell Homes public housing developments in Atlanta.

furnish tenants with supportive social services. HOU provides information and referrals on jobs and educational opportunities. It handles the recreational programming and counsels families on budgeting, housekeeping, and the importance of paying rent. Parents who fail to control unruly children are brought in for private conferences and given help on a one-to-one basis.

The cost of these services averages about $30 per unit per year, though initial costs may be higher. For instance, during the first few years, the per-unit costs of HOU's services at the Harbor Point development in Boston averaged $100 per unit. The cost is written in as a line item in the budget and is covered by rental income, although HOU often brings in other resources, like programs or grants, to supplement its own services.

Corcoran notes that security generally is an issue for the first few years, and security measures typically cost about $100 per unit per year, as at Harbor Point. Eventually, management stabilizes the development, and the security program is phased out gradually. Another view on security comes from Tom Costello: "Try to avoid offering a special security program. It's expensive and gives the perception that you have problems." Instead, McCormack Baron sometimes offers discounts to police officers interested in moving into their developments.

Because its projects typically involve the redevelopment of troubled low-income properties, one of the major challenges for the Corcoran Jennison Companies is to convince existing residents that promises of a better environment will be fulfilled. Thus, the firm works in partnership with community residents during the development process and in the management of the communities. It identifies respected leaders within the community and encourages them to take on management roles.

Richard Baron counsels that "all housing should be managed as though it was market-rate." At McCormack Baron, management procedures include yearly home inspections (at the time leases are renegotiated), prompt fulfillment of work orders, and a commitment to good service. Management asks that maintenance personnel report—and correct—any problems at once. The firm insists on prompt rent payments and collects rents through lockboxes.

For mixed-income developments to work, management must be tough in enforcing rules and collecting rents. This approach should apply equally to all tenants, low-income and market-rate, previ-ous residents and newcomers. Problem families must be evicted if they cannot comply. Otherwise, the project will go downhill very quickly.

# Transformation of Public Housing into Mixed-Income Communities

Many of the nation's most distressed public housing developments are found in inner-city neighborhoods and have contributed to the decline of their surroundings. In cities throughout the United States, some of the worst of these developments are being transformed into mixed-income communities, in many cases with the participation of a for-profit private developer.

The purpose of public housing in the United States is to provide decent shelter for low-income households. Much of the public housing stock is well run and provides low-income families with a good place to live. Nonetheless, in cities throughout the country, severely distressed public housing developments blight communities with their crumbling buildings, deteriorating streets, boarded-up units, trash, graffiti, and myriad social problems. Efforts are now underway by the U.S. Department of Housing and Urban Development (HUD), local public housing authorities (PHAs), and their various public and private partners to transform these eyesores into developments that will help improve the life chances of the families who live there and that will be assets to the communities where they are located.

### The HOPE VI Program

HUD hopes to stimulate the revitalization of severely distressed public housing developments, largely through its HOPE VI program, which is also known as the Urban Revitalization Demonstration (URD) program or, as of 1996, the Severely Distressed Public Housing initiative. HOPE VI has provided flexible federal funding to spur the holistic revitalization of public housing developments, typically through physical improvements, economic integration, and the provision of supportive and community services. And the program encourages the creation of public/private partnerships to undertake this work. The most important desired result is the integration of public housing residents, units, and public housing communities into the mainstream of American life.

Because HUD recognizes that real change in the lives of residents will not result from physical improvements alone, up to 20 percent of HOPE VI grant money can be used for the provision of community and supportive services for residents. The program allows flexibility in the use of funds; encourages PHAs to leverage the funds through mixed-financing arrangements; and promotes the forming of public/private partnerships with residents, nonprofit and for-profit developers, the city, and other players in the affordable housing delivery system. It also encourages mixed-income developments, which have become a realistic option since HUD ruled that public housing units can be privately owned if the housing authority ensures compliance with the public housing law.

Although much of the current mixed-income development activity involving public housing units is centered around the HOPE VI program, some developments built before this program was initiated and others underway have gotten their primary funding from other sources, typically from HUD public housing development funds. (The primary difference between HOPE VI and other programs is that HOPE VI allows a portion of the program funds to be used for community and supportive services. Development funds also impose more limits on allowable per-unit development costs than does HOPE VI.)

The goals in recreating public housing developments as mixed-income communities are to:

- End the isolation of public housing residents from mainstream society.
- End the isolation of public housing developments from the larger community.
- End the isolation of public housing authorities from the local affordable housing delivery system.
- Relieve concentrations of poverty.
- Remove and replace badly deteriorated and poorly designed public housing.
- Provide decent housing for public-housing-eligible families and others in high-quality living environments.
- Create developments that can be sustained over time.
- Make public housing a benefit rather than a blight to the larger community.

In addition, HUD would like the HOPE VI program to help improve PHAs' management of public housing developments, to make PHAs more entrepreneurial and efficient, to encourage them to tap into the existing resource of private sector development and management expertise, and to encourage them to leverage federal funds (to ac-commodate the anticipated long-term reductions in federal funding).

## Project Examples

A number of projects of this kind are now underway throughout the country. The following are but a few illustrative examples:

*Techwood/Clark Howell Homes, Atlanta.* Techwood and Clark Howell Homes, adjacent to the Olympic Village in Atlanta, orginally consisted of 1,100 public housing units in 41 buildings. The buildings were demolished in May 1995 and will be replaced over the next four years with 900 housing units in the form of townhouses and garden apartments. Forty percent of the units will be public housing, 20 percent will be for households within the limits set by the federal low-income housing tax credit (LIHTC) program,[2] and 40 percent will be market-rate units. Fourteen units will be set aside for use in social service and economic development programs. The resulting Village of Techwood will also include a community services center, a new elementary school, restoration of the vacant Carnegie public library, and recreational facilities that will encompass basketball courts, tennis courts, and a swimming pool. Community residents are helping to design a comprehensive array of social services.

A joint venture partnership of The Integral Partnership of Atlanta—composed of The Integral Group, LLC, of Atlanta, and McCormack Baron Associates, Inc., of St. Louis—serves as the project manager and master developer. The Atlanta Housing Authority is responsible for demolition and site preparation and for relocating existing residents. The city of Atlanta will make needed infrastructure improvements.

The first phase of the Techwood project closed in February 1996.

*Vaughn, St. Louis.* The George L. Vaughn Family Apartments, built in 1957 one block from the infamous Pruitt-Igoe public housing development, included 656 units in four nine-story buildings. The buildings have been demolished, and a new development, The Residences at Murphy Park, is now being built. Plans include a mixed-income neighborhood of 402 units, 222 of which will be public housing units. Phase I will include 160 units, including 93 public housing units, 25 LIHTC units, and 42 market-rate ones. Structures will include townhouses, garden apartments, and detached houses. Variety in styling, materials, and colors will make for individuality; porches, patios, and individual entries will form private spaces. Amenities will include a daycare center, pool and deck, tot lots, and three new small city parks.

The St. Louis Housing Authority received a special set-aside of public housing development funds in the Cranston-Gonzalez National Affordable Housing Act of 1992 to demolish the 1957 project and to develop a demonstration program on the site. Phase I will cost $17.4 million, of which approximately $9.1 million will be public housing development funds, $3.4 million private equity investment, and $2.5 million corporate donations. The Missouri Housing Development Commission is providing a $2.2 million FHA-insured first mortgage, as well as $0.5 million in LIHTC and $1.4 million in state affordable housing credits for the annual corporate donations. The project is being aided by investments from corporate partners that include Anheuser-Busch, Southwestern Bell, and Mercantile Bank. The city of St. Louis is providing $1.65 million in public improvements and a real estate tax abatement.

The St. Louis Housing Authority will retain ownership of the site and will lease it to the development partnership. Phase I will be owned by a limited partnership comprising the St. Louis Housing Authority, Vaughn Tenant Association, Carr Square Tenant Corporation, Cochran Gardens Tenant Management Corporation, and McCormack Baron & Associates, Inc.

*East Lake Meadows, Atlanta.* Another Atlanta transformation project, The New Community at East Lake, is an interesting example of how a foundation—in partnership with the corporate community, residents, and the local housing authority—is exploiting the economic power of golf to rebuild East Lake Meadows, a 650-unit deteriorated public housing project. The East Lake Community Foundation (ELCF), a public charitable foundation affiliated with the CF Foundation, is working in partnership with public and private organizations[3] to develop the housing, other physical facilities, and community programs. ELCF has helped to assemble a 170-acre site (of which 55 acres was the original public housing site) and, in partnership with the Atlanta Housing Authority, to write plans for a new mixed-income community. Half of the planned 500 units will be public housing, and half will be available at market rates. Community amenities will include a new public 18-hole golf course, tennis courts, parks, nature trails, a family YMCA, a preschool, and an elementary school. Working closely with residents and public and private partners, ELCF will also develop, fund, and operate a wide range of community educational and recreational programs, including a junior golf academy.

East Lake Golf Club, famous as Bobby Jones's home course, is located just across the street from the development site. The CF Foundation bought and restored the golf club with the help of corporate contributions. Corporations that join the golf club are the primary sources of funds for the amenities in the new mixed-income development at East Lake Meadows. Each corporation will be asked to support the redevelopment effort through charitable donations of at least $200,000 each. The golf club also will contribute its surplus cash flows to the East Lake Community Foundation to support the educational and recreational programs.

HUD is providing $32.5 million in public housing development funds for on-site and replacement public housing units; and private developers are matching that amount to finance the market-rate housing. ELCF and the Atlanta Housing Authority will be responsible for developing the housing, while ELCF will develop and manage the public golf course and tennis center and will fund the YMCA.

*Ellen Wilson Dwellings, Washington, D.C.* Ellen Wilson Dwellings is an abandoned public housing development on Capitol Hill in Washington, D.C., that consists of 134 housing units in 13 buildings on a 5.3-acre site. Revitalization plans call for the construction of 134 units of limited-equity cooperative units, 19 fee-simple homeownership units, and a community center, daycare center, and park. Resident preferences will determine which supportive services are provided, but these will involve the work of an on-site services coordinator.

Fee-simple units will be market-rate. Co-op units will be allocated among four income bands: (1) 33 units for households earning zero to 25 percent of the median income; (2) 34 units for those earning 25 to 50 percent; (3) 47 units for those earning 50 to 80 percent; and (4) 20 units for those earning 80 to 115 percent of the median income. The project will be developed by two for-profit developers, Corcoran Jennison Companies and Telesis Corporation, in partnership with the nonprofit Ellen Wilson Neighborhood Redevelopment Corporation, a community development corporation composed of residents from all parts of the community surrounding the Ellen Wilson site, including former residents of the public housing project.

*Spring View Apartments, San Antonio.* Spring View Apartments is a distressed, partly vacant,

The former Vaughn public housing project in St. Louis is being reborn as The Residences at Murphy Park.

421-unit public housing development on 50 acres on San Antonio's largely African American East Side. Its transformation plans emphasize a holistic approach, with particular attention to ensuring the provision of needed services. Revitalization plans call for the demolition of the units and the construction of a mixed-income community of single-family houses, townhouses, and apartments, including a full range of social and community services to be provided in cooperation with area service providers and nearby institutions; plus community facilities to include a community recreation center, ballfields, parkland, and a horticultural/garden center.

To make public housing residence a stepping-stone to independence, families in public housing units must participate in the HUD Family Self-Sufficiency Program, which provides training, skill development support resources, and social support services to enable participants to achieve agreed-upon goals. The housing authority will implement its plan by leveraging a $48.8 million HOPE VI grant.

*First Ward Place, Charlotte, North Carolina.* First Ward Place, located in the First Ward neighborhood in uptown Charlotte, North Carolina, is another HOPE VI grantee that is emphasizing community services. Plans call for a combination of rehabilitation and new construction to yield 350 housing units: 132 for public-housing-eligible families, 50 for families with incomes up to 60 percent of the median, 68 for the elderly, and 100 at market rates. The community will be developed by NationsBank Community Development Corporation in partnership with the Charlotte Housing Authority.

Through its pioneering Family Self-Sufficiency Program, the Charlotte Housing Authority intends to create "an incubator for future homeowners"— a community within which public housing residents can eventually hope to own their own homes. To reside in First Ward Place, low-income tenants must agree to work or go to school and must agree, in writing, to work their way out of subsidized housing within three years. Through a plan that saves any increases in rent payments for the family, low-income renters can become homeowners and can mentor other families in the self-sufficiency program.

The project has been designed as a mix of new construction and rehabilitation. Plans include a community plaza, daycare, a community service center, and space for future commercial or mixed-use development.

*Hayes Valley, San Francisco.* Hayes Valley is a mixed-income, mixed-use project in San Francisco's Western Addition that involves the demolition of 294 public-housing garden apartments

and the rebuilding of 195 townhouses designed for large families. Sixty percent of the units will be set aside for public-housing-eligible families, and the remaining 40 percent for tax-credit-eligible households. The project is being developed by McCormack Baron & Associates, The Related Companies, the San Francisco Housing Authority, and the Hayes Valley Resident Management Corporation. Units offer garages, washers and dryers, a computer network linking all units within the development, and 3,000 square feet of retail space operated by the tenants.

## Creating New Mixed-Income Communities That Contain Public Housing

According to Meg Sowell, president of Real Estate Strategies, Inc., in Wayne, Pennsylvania, determining the market for a mixed-income, inner-city project that includes public housing can be difficult. As Sowell has discussed in Chapter 2, she recommends supplementing the demographic and income data typically used in a market analysis with location-specific information on buying and renting patterns and with a profile of the types of households interested in the location. For example, in researching the market for the Ellen Wilson site in Washington, D.C., her firm interviewed realtors and developers active in the project's immediate area; commissioned focus groups with area residents; identified and analyzed realistic comparable developments; and, based on the nature of current demand, drew a profile of the likely target market for the unsubsidized portion

of the proposed development: upscale urban singles and couples who are executives or professionals, and students. Sowell's market analysis helped confirm the viability of a proposal to redevelop the project as a limited-equity co-op and to refine project plans to fit the realities of the market.

As with other mixed-income communities, the community design and unit design should be planned in the same way as they would be for a market-rate property, and the result should look like a high-quality residential development. Designs should of course be functional and durable but should also be beautiful: "Architecture conveys signals that do nearly as much as the cost of rent and location to determine whether people will live there."[4] Columns on porches, white picket fences, and other touches convey architecturally a sense of pride and dignity. The character of the development and the quality of the housing units can, to a large extent, change the public perception of a community.[5]

To help overcome the traditional isolation of public housing within the neighborhood, the new community should be designed to weave into the larger community fabric. Its homes should be compatible in scale, arrangement, materials, and architecture with the neighborhood context; and the patterns of streets and open space should knit the development seamlessly into its surroundings. Plans for the revitalization of Pittsburgh's Allequippa Terrace public housing development include a major redesign of its street plans, to connect the new community to the surrounding neighborhood. And the site plan for the revitalized Ellen Wilson Dwellings will integrate the new community into the existing neighborhood fabric through connecting streets, and architecture (and infrastructure) that will meet the standards of the nearby Capitol Hill Historic District. For example, townhouse design will be based on the typical Capitol Hill rowhouse, and all sidewalks will be made of brick.

Integrating public housing developments with surrounding neighborhoods also means replacing high-rise buildings with smaller-scale units (single-family houses, townhouses, and garden apartments), developing on small blocks, and setting up a hierarchy of streets and green spaces. Designs today commonly include rowhouse buildings with private yards, limited-access interior courtyards, and stronger connections between buildings and streets. The objective is to afford a more middle-class appearance so as to enable the development to blend into the surrounding neighborhood and appeal to market-rate residents.

At the same time, multifamily elevator buildings in mixed-income settings can be very attractive to market-rate renters and small households of adult, low-income families. Multifamily buildings can also enable more innovation in the use of land, allow more open space, and, on difficult sites, make possible the provision of more units that are accessible to persons with physical disabilities.

Because safety is such a key concern in this type of development, defensible design principles should be incorporated wherever possible. These include promoting resident surveillance by designing homes with windows and porches that face the street, using see-through fencing, lining the perimeters of parks with streets for maximum visibility, lighting streets and buildings, and minimizing unsupervised space within multifamily buildings. Unsupervised space between buildings should also be eliminated; instead, open space between units should take the form of front- and backyards that are controlled and maintained by individual residents. In addition, streets should be designed to discourage nonresident through-traffic, for example, by making them narrow, inserting stop signs, and limiting entryways.

Community designs must include facilities and amenities that are appropriate to the market to be served, both for livability reasons and also to make the project competitive in the local market. Existing public housing residents can be valuable members of the design team. During the planning of the East Lake Meadows development, residents were invited to review preliminary plans and propose their own design recommendations. A number of residents' proposals resulted in changes that improved the plan.

There is no general agreement on what constitutes an ideal income mix for these types of developments. Factors to consider include the site's location, local market conditions, the needs and desires of existing public housing and community residents, and the requirements associated with financing. According to Richard Baron, "Our experience in nonpublic-housing, mixed-income developments is that it is always a matter of values and not of incomes. If the families want to live in that community, and there's good screening and site management, they will live together very well." But he goes on to add that he believes that 60 percent is the maximum share of public housing units for a viable mix. In addition, the number of units overall must be large enough to make an impact on the market in a community. Baron suggests 150 units as the minimum number for a public housing transformation.

Most observers believe that, to end the isolation and stigma associated with public housing residency, public housing units in mixed-income developments should be interspersed among and indistinguishable from the other subsidized units and from market-rate units. Intermingling of public and private units can be accomplished through an agreement between the housing authority and HUD, such as the one executed for The Village at Techwood. HUD has agreed to allow public housing operating subsidies that are not attached to particular units; instead, they "float" with the public housing family.

Locating public housing residents within a mixed-income environment, especially where subsidies are not attached to particular units, gives people a real incentive to improve their situations. Public housing residents pay up to 30 percent of their incomes on rent. As a resident's income increases, at some point it will be possible for her or him to rent a tax-credit unit rather than a public housing unit. Within these new mixed-income developments with "floating" public housing units, moving out of public housing does not require moving out of one's home. (To maintain the required number of public housing units, if a public housing tenant shifts to renting a tax-credit unit instead, the next available unit will be designated as public housing.)

Including homeownership opportunities in the development—particularly for public housing residents—fosters stability, pride, and a sense of stewardship on the part of public housing residents. To enable public housing residents to aspire to owning their homes, homeownership counseling and programs should form part of the transformation plan.

Financing for these developments is highly project-specific and is perhaps the major determinant in project planning. As with any other development that includes low-income housing, financing is dependent on government programs. Today, most, though not all, public housing transformations into mixed-income developments rely on HOPE VI funds. To accomplish their goals at a time when federal money for low-income housing is decreasing—a trend that is expected to continue—PHAs also need to leverage public funds with private money. HOPE VI funds are typically leveraged with money from CDBGs, LIHTCs, HUD HOME program funds, taxable and tax-exempt bonds, state and local program funds, and private sources of financing. Some of the factors affecting how a given development is financed will include the choice of the population(s) to be served, the local real estate tax environment, the role chosen by the housing authority, the availability of LIHTCs, and the availability of tax-exempt bonds.[6]

The Village at Techwood, for example, is financed through equity from LIHTCs, a first mortgage from the FHA, and a second mortgage from the Atlanta Housing Authority through a HOPE VI grant for the construction of public housing units. Because the money is loaned to the partnership, in 55 years, when the second mortgage is paid off, the money will be repaid and recycled. A $250,000 financing gap was filled by leasing parts of the site for use during the Olympic Games.

The Vaughn project in St. Louis was based on almost the same model as Techwood but used public housing development funds, while also relying on waiver requests to take advantage of features available programmatically through HOPE VI. Both Techwood and Vaughn involved almost two years of close collaboration among HUD, the PHAs, and the developers. Both featured FHA-insured first mortgages, housing-authority soft second mortgages and grants, tax-credit equity, private ownership in the form of a limited partnership, long-term land leases to the partnerships by the PHAs, and private management. The documents and processes developed for Techwood and Vaughn have become prototypes for mixed-finance, mixed-income developments.[7]

Marketing and leasing techniques will be the same as for any market-rate community, with these cautions: to market a transformed public housing development as a mixed-income community, the new community must offer high-quality housing products at prices that represent a good value and amenities that compete well with other, similarly priced developments in the market. Market-rate buyers should feel that they are getting a bargain within that market. And any negative image or stigma attached to the previous public housing development must be erased by the large and highly visible physical transformation and by the market's perception that the development is a privately developed new community, not a rebuilt public housing project. As Baron explains, "The approach is not building a traditional public housing development that happens to have market-rate units in it; rather, it is building a market-rate community that has public housing units in it."

One of the challenges for PHAs in this era of declining federal funding is to create developments whose revenues will cover costs and yet yield some surplus to help defray their administrative expenses. Unlike turnkey or traditional public housing developments, public housing transformations typically involve PHAs as participating partners. As such, PHAs will receive the negotiated portion of the upfront fees and the income stream from the nonpublic housing units, as well as income from the public housing units.

The community must be managed in the same way as any well-managed private rental community, which means that both manager and tenants must meet their responsibilities fully and on time. Many PHAs have not been good managers of rental properties; these authorities should contract with experienced private management companies for that function.

As with other mixed-income developments, tenant screening is particularly important in mixed-income communities that include public housing. And because security is such an important goal, management must be willing to evict undesirable tenants. The Clinton administration's "one strike and you're out" rule enables PHAs to screen tenants, enforce lease provisions, and evict families whose members are involved in drug deals or other criminal activity. In addition, through Operation Safe Home, HUD is working with local law enforcement agencies to eliminate gang activity and violent crime. Other programs encourage community policing, foster crime prevention programs, and discourage drug use.

Good maintenance and management are essential to the long-term sustainability of the new community, as with any housing development. Keeping the community safe, clean, and fiscally sound will require resident cooperation and participation. Homeowners' and residents' associations and the involvement of residents in community management decisions are good vehicles for building a sense of ownership and shared responsibility for the community. Homeowners' associations should be encouraged to adopt a design review process to evaluate any proposed modifications to the homes and should require minimum home maintenance practices.

Where public housing transformation developments are located within neighborhoods that are themselves distressed, revitalization plans must include strategies for improving those neighborhoods through housing rehabilitation, infrastructure repair, improved public services, and other means.

Public housing residents will likely object to the planned new mixed-income development at first. Even the most distressed development, for the people who live there, is home. Many tenants have lived in the development for years and have a strong sense of community. Residents often fear that change, and particularly demolition, will deprive them of their homes, change the character of their community, introduce newcomers with whom they will not be comfortable, and, in the case of some individuals, threaten their power base. Fear of displacement is especially acute in public housing developments located in areas that are attractive for private investment.

Wary, too, of changing ideas about welfare, public housing residents may feel especially vulnerable. And people will have an agenda: they will be concerned over who will have priority for the new housing; some may want to participate in the selection of the developer and property manager; and some may want specific action items, such as job creation or economic development opportunities. Because of their stakes in the outcomes, residents must be involved in every stage of the revitalization effort.

## Structuring a Public/Private Partnership

Through the HOPE VI program, HUD is encouraging the formation of public/private partnerships for the transformation of public housing developments. But the interplay between public agencies and private developers has not always been easy.

Past experience in working together has included the urban renewal, Urban Development Action Grant (UDAG), Section 235 and 236, Section 8, and FHA coinsurance programs. The public sector typically suspects that developers make too much money (though there are no standards for what is a fair profit), and private developers chafe under the myriad rules and regulations that characterize public sector activity. The result has been a love-hate relationship, and the challenge is to craft a partnership to accomplish mutual goals.

A public/private partnership model, often employed by Corcoran Jennison Companies, is for the developer to enter into a joint venture with the residents' council to lease a property from the housing authority for a long time (typically 99 years). The joint venture develops, owns, and operates the project, yet the housing authority can ensure that the development achieves the intended public purpose through conditions attached to the lease that specify the number of units to be used for public housing, income limits, admission criteria and procedures, and so forth. In addition, to ensure continuing compliance, the housing authority typically inserts continued reporting and monitoring requirements into the lease agreement. This model, according to Marty Jones, president of Corcoran Jennison Companies in Boston, "brings the residents to the table as decisionmakers, not just advisers. It's not patronizing."

Where private developers lease land from PHAs and construct and operate the new developments, PHAs benefit from these public/private partnerships through the development of public housing units, with public housing dollars, as part of a larger community. The public housing units operate on a break-even basis but support no debt service. The PHA can share in the cash flow generated by the nonpublic housing units and can devote these additional resources toward preserving the viability of the public housing units and providing vital community and supportive services.

At the same time, PHAs must adjust to new ways of doing business. The project will be privately developed and privately run; applicants will come to an on-site leasing facility rather than to the housing authority. There will be a site-based waiting list. Yet the PHA will still own the land, which it will lease with a nonforecloseable land use restriction; it will lend funds to the project, and it will regulate that portion of the project that receives its operating subsidies.

# Westminster Place, St. Louis, Missouri

Westminster Place in St. Louis features a wide variety of housing types, including for-sale, single-family houses.

Westminster Place is an example of a large-scale, mixed-income development that has successfully re-created a viable community in a deteriorated city neighborhood.

## Project Background

Westminster Place, a 12-block mixed-income community, has been under development for the past 11 years in the city of St. Louis. The 90-acre redevelopment area is located in a corridor between the city's Midtown and the historic Central West End that saw widespread disinvestment, blight, and outmigration during the 1970s and early 1980s. Liquor stores and pawn shops occupied the few remaining streetfronts. One main intersection that was once part of the Gaslight Square district came to

be called "the Stroll" because it was the city's best-known haven for prostitution and drug dealing.

In 1983, the city approved McCormack Baron's master plan for the 90-acre redevelopment area. The city's aspirations were to stem the crime and deterioration in the area, as well as to stabilize this central land parcel, which threatened to disrupt the steady revitalization of two adjacent neighborhoods: St. Louis University to the south, and the Central West End.

The onetime wasteland of vacant lots and scarred buildings now supports a neighborhood of some 1,000 residents with tree-lined sidewalks, wide streets, a community swimming pool, and a shopping center. Westminster Place is representative of the type of large-scale, mixed-income communities

that McCormack Baron is developing in distressed downtowns around the country. The Westminster neighborhood offers nearly 400 housing units: two-story, Colonial-style, brick-and-frame rental garden apartments; attached rental townhouses; attached two-family homes; and 35 for-sale, single-family houses. Some two-thirds of the redevelopment had been completed as of early 1997, and an additional 20 to 25 single-family houses will be built in 1997 through 1998.

In summer 1997, construction started on a 96-unit, assisted-living facility for seniors. Financed largely with federal low-income housing tax credits, three-quarters of the apartments will be set aside for low-income tenants. There is no other facility like this one in the area. It is envisioned that some aging residents of other St. Louis McCormack Baron developments, who are no longer capable of living independently but do not yet require nursing-home care, will eventually move here.

Household incomes at Westminster Place encompass a broad range. Some residents live on fixed incomes with federal Section 8 vouchers. Thirty-six percent of households earn between $10,000 and $20,000, while 18 percent earn from $40,000 to as much as $165,000. The median household income is around $47,000. The central location, convenient to several major employment centers, has been a significant draw for the market-rate development. Likewise, suburban-type amenities such as attached garages, washers and dryers, and a community pool have also attracted residents to the neighborhood.

## Financing

In the first development phase, McCormack Baron teamed with a commercial developer to build an adjacent 145,000-square-foot shopping center to support the burgeoning residential neighborhood. Developed in three phases and financed partially with federal Urban Development Action Grants (UDAGs), the center features a full-service grocery store, a managed health care facility, and an assortment of retail shops, many of which are minority-managed businesses.

Most of the project equity was raised from the syndication of federal low-income housing tax credits (LIHTCs). The rest came from federal and state grants, local charities, and the sale of tax-exempt bonds. A local bank made an advantageous mortgage loan for the first phase of development. The low-income senior living facility has been financed primarily through LIHTCs and funds from the State of Missouri Affordable Housing Assistance Program, a program that mimics federal LIHTCs.

## Related Development

Westminster Place has recently attracted a number of other developments, including a low-income seniors' housing complex built by a nonprofit religious group; a Mormon church; the administrative offices of the American Cancer Society; and a new magnet school. Metro High, known as "the Bronx Science of the St. Louis public schools," opened here last fall. Richard Baron worked with the St. Louis Board of Education to obtain special neighborhood preference designations so that at least 15 percent of the slots would be reserved for children residing in the neighborhood. Before this designation, neighborhood schoolchildren who wanted to attend magnet schools had to participate in a lottery and usually ended up at schools across town—a situation that had discouraged families with young children from moving to Westminster Place.

*Source:* From a *ULI Project Reference File* report by Terry Lassar, to be published online in January 1998.

# Del Norte Place, El Cerrito, California

Separate entryways and parking spaces for the retail and residential portions of the project assure privacy and security for the residents of Del Norte Place.

Del Norte Place is an example of an innovative transit-oriented, mixed-use, mixed-income infill development.

The development is a 135-unit, four-story apartment project with 21,000 square feet of ground-floor retail space. The project features an updated Mediterranean design, ground-level retail, and market-rate, affordable, and seniors' housing units. Located one block from a Bay Area Rapid Transit (BART) station, the $18.8 million project provides an alternative to automobile commuting that is used by almost half of its residents. Twenty percent of the units are allocated to seniors, and 20

percent go to low-income households.

The 4.1-acre Del Norte site once contained a run-down motel, a variety of boarded-up commercial buildings, and several vacant parcels. The site fronted on a major north/south commercial thoroughfare and was bounded at the rear by the elevated BART tracks. The site was assembled from 13 separate parcels by the redevelopment agency, which also managed the relocation of five businesses and six dwelling units.

To develop the site, an electric distribution substation had to be relocated; a portion of a street running through the site

had to be vacated; and some of the soils, which had proven deficient, had to be replaced. Adjacent to the site were several other buildings and vacant parcels, which only now—after Del Norte Place has successfully pioneered the area—are being developed.

## Design and Architecture

Del Norte's 135 apartments are located in four buildings, each with its own entrance and elevator system. The two center buildings are joined at the base. Commercial spaces are located on the street side of the ground floor of each building and open onto a broad, metal-roofed arcade. Retail parking is found in front of the two center buildings, and residential parking runs the length of the site at the rear, underneath the BART trestles.

Though market studies had indicated that adherence to standard parking requirements would not be necessary at Del Norte Place, the code-mandated number of parking spaces was provided, principally at the insistence of the city council. The residential units now have overabundant parking, but the overage has proven helpful in accommodating retail parking needs at peak hours.

The buildings are designed in the Mediterranean style, with updated elements. The terra cotta–colored, metal standing-seam roof of the ground-floor retail arcade is supported on wooden "Tuscan" columns. Above the arcade, the residential facades are clad in stucco of varying earth tones, punctuated by deep balcony recesses. Capping the composition is a standing-seam metal mansard roof, echoing the roof of the arcade below. A further sense of articulation is provided by the stepped massing of the facades and by the fireplace chimneys' projection above the roofline.

Residential units, which are conventionally wood-framed, sit on a post-tensioned, concrete-slab podium over the retail level. The slab was engineered with an eye toward maximum flexibility for the ground-floor retail uses; the number of required supporting columns was minimized, and locations for slab openings for restaurant exhaust ventilation shafts were provided.

The residential buildings were designed to be as open and individual as possible, to minimize the institutional quality often found in similar buildings. Each of the four buildings has single-loaded exterior balcony corridors around a landscaped courtyard. In the courtyards are seating areas and storage facilities for bicycles and outdoor equipment. Other amenities include a weight room and spa, a meeting room, and a tot lot.

Seniors' units are all in one building. Additional amenities for elderly residents include a separate "senior commons" social/meeting room, an emergency pull-cord system in each dwelling unit, and an older adults' medical clinic.

The 27 affordable units are dispersed throughout the project, and all apartment types and locations, except the top-floor fireplace units, are available to low-income tenants.

## Ownership and Financing

The project's developer is the Ibex Group, a California partnership that includes The John Stewart Company, as well as the principals from Sandy & Babcock, Inc., the architect of Del Norte Place, and Midstate Construction, the builder of the complex. The Ibex Group is the general partner of the Del Norte Place Limited Partnership, which owns the project. Leasing and management are provided by The John Stewart Company.

The site for Del Norte Place, which was acquired for $3 million by the El Cerrito Redevelopment Agency through the issuance of "qualified redevelopment bonds," is leased to the project owner for a period of 65 years. The redevelopment agency in return will receive 20 percent of the net project cash flow (after the fifth year) and a 20 percent share of eventual sale proceeds.

Construction and permanent financing of approximately $11 million was provided through 40-year, fixed-rate, tax-exempt mortgage revenue bonds issued by Contra Costa County. These funds were refinanced in 1994 in favor of a lower-interest, variable-rate, tax-exempt bond indexed to the seven-day Kenny Index. The loan proceeds were insured through the FHA coinsurance program, 221(d)(4), which gives the bonds a GNMA guarantee and thus a superior bond rating.

The principal source of the remaining funds was equity provided by the Del Norte Place Limited Partnership. The Ibex Group, as general partner, contributed roughly $3.2 million. Low-income housing tax credits were syndicated to 30 individual limited partners for another $1.8 million in equity contributions. Additionally, the Contra Costa County Department of Community Development provided $200,000 through the CDBG program.

The tenant profile is diverse. Forty-seven percent of the residents are employed, 43 percent are retirees, and 10 percent are university students. Thirty-nine percent of residents are over 62 years of age; 8 percent are aged 52 to 62; 6 percent are 46 to 55; 16 percent are 36 to 45; 17 percent are 26 to 35; and 14 percent are 18 to 25 years old. About two-thirds of tenants moved to the development from another apartment. Just over half of the residents do not own cars. Forty-eight percent travel to work by rapid transit.

# Del Norte Place Project Data

## Land Use Information

Site Area: 4.1 acres
Total Dwelling Units: 135
Gross Density: 33 units per acre
Off-Street Parking Spaces: 234 (retail and residential)

## Land Use Plan

| | Acres | Percent of Site |
|---|---|---|
| Buildings | 1.24 | 30 |
| Roads/Paved Areas | 2.15 | 52 |
| Common Open Space | 0.48 | 12 |
| Retail Arcade | 0.23 | 6 |
| Total | 4.10 | 100 |

## Residential Information

| Unit Type(Square Feet) | Unit Size | Number of Units Planned/ Built | Range of Initial Rents |
|---|---|---|---|
| Market-Rate | 810 | 92/92 | $900–1,000 |
| Seniors' | 552 | 16/16 | $800–875 |
| Affordable[1] | 732 | 27/27 | $500–550 |

## Development Cost Information

| | Residential Only | Retail Only | Total |
|---|---|---|---|
| Site Acquisition Cost | $2,550,000 | $450,000 | $3,000,000 |
| Site Improvement Costs | | | |
| Demolition | $65,532 | $11,564 | $77,096 |
| Grading/sewer/walks | 67,952 | 11,991 | 79,943 |
| Asbestos removal | 78,142 | 13,790 | 91,932 |
| Utility relocation | 103,297 | 18,229 | 121,256 |
| Total | $314,922 | $55,575 | $370,497 |
| Construction Costs | | | |
| Superstructure | $9,056,142 | $1,598,143 | $10,654,285 |
| Inspection and testing | 55,250 | 9,750 | 65,000 |
| Permits and fees | 276,378 | 48,773 | 325,150 |
| Performance bond | 64,355 | 11,357 | 75,712 |
| Total | $9,452,125 | $1,668,022 | $11,120,147 |

## Soft Costs

| | | | |
|---|---|---|---|
| Architecture/engineering | $701,767 | $123,841 | $825,608 |
| Technical consultants | 53,213 | 9,390 | 62,603 |
| Development management | 46,750 | 8,250 | 55,000 |
| Market analysis | 29,313 | 5,173 | 34,486 |
| Legal | 58,319 | 10,292 | 68,611 |
| Marketing/retail commissions | 250,300 | 44,171 | 294,471 |
| Taxes and insurance | 63,750 | 11,250 | 75,000 |
| LC fees/bond issuance | 336,569 | 59,394 | 395,963 |
| Construction loan interest | 634,376 | 111,949 | 746,325 |
| Construction/permanent loan fees | 498,601 | 87,988 | 586,589 |
| Syndication of tax credits | 26,350 | 4,650 | 31,000 |
| Retail T.I. allowance | 425,000 | 75,000 | 500,000 |
| Contingency | 527,700 | 93,000 | 620,000 |
| Total | $3,651,308 | $644,348 | $4,295,656 |
| Total Development Cost | $15,968,355 | $2,817,945 | $18,786,300 |

Total Development Cost per Residential Unit: $118,284
(not including land—per cash flow to agency): $99,395
Total Cost per Retail Unit (i.e., est. 12 spaces): $234,829
(not including land—per cash flow to agency): $197,329

## Annual Operating Expenses

| Expenses | Residential | Retail[2] | Total |
|---|---|---|---|
| Taxes | $100,000 | $20,000 | $120,000 |
| Insurance | 30,000 | 5,000 | 35,000 |
| Services | 15,000 | 15,000 | 30,000 |
| Maintenance | 120,000 | 22,500 | 142,500 |
| Janitorial | 25,000 | 10,000 | 35,000 |
| Utilities | 50,000 | 15,000 | 65,000 |
| Legal | 10,000 | 0 | 10,000 |
| Management | 115,000 | 10,000 | 125,000 |
| Miscellaneous | 7,500 | 2,500 | 10,000 |
| Total | $472,500 | $100,000 | $572,500 |

1. Rent is set at 30 percent of 50 percent of Contra Costa County median income.

2. Retail: Common-areas maintenance (CAM) charges average $0.42 per net rentable square foot per month.

*Source:* Excerpted from *ULI Project Reference File* report, Volume 25, Number 10.

# Homan Square, Chicago, Illinois

The Homan Square development is a large, mixed-income residential project being built in a distressed urban neighborhood. It has been designed to create a more diverse residential base and to improve the neighborhood environment, making it more attractive to additional private investment.

The Shaw Company, with Sears, Roebuck & Company as its financial partner, is developing a new community of 600 single-family, attached, and apartment homes on the 55-acre former Sears headquarters site in the North Lawndale neighborhood of Chicago. The

project will also include the renovation of 1 million square feet of existing commercial buildings and the development of parks, gardens, and open space. The commercial development is expected to generate business and employment opportunities for residents, and the project will create approximately 3,000 new jobs. The Shaw Company will also facilitate the provision of a comprehensive array of community services.

The development goal is to recreate a stable, secure, economically integrated neighborhood. The development partner-

ship also intends and expects Homan Square to be a catalyst for the revitalization of other sections of the North Lawndale community.

Development will occur in phases. Construction began in February 1994 and will continue through 1999.

## The Site

Named for Homan Avenue, a major street that traverses the site, Homan Square is located on the city's West Side less than five miles from downtown Chicago in North Lawndale, a low-income, largely minority

Phase I of Homan Square, 600 units of single-family, attached, and multifamily homes, has been completed. Among the units are 24 subsidized single-family houses and 50 rental units (20 townhouses and five buildings of six flats each). The long-term goal is to offer tenants the opportunity to buy their units.

neighborhood that has lost 60 percent of its population during the past 30 years. Physical and social problems abound. Housing abandonment is widespread here, and half of the land is vacant. About 40 percent of working-age adults are unemployed.

The Shaw Company nevertheless believed that the site was well located for a new, large-scale, mixed-income housing development. Housing immediately adjacent to the site is relatively stable, with less vacancy. The site is just a quick commute to downtown Chicago via a nearby Chicago Transit Authority stop or by way of the Eisenhower Expressway, and it is near two large public parks: Douglas Park and Garfield Park, which is currently being redeveloped. Nearby neighborhoods have recently been revitalized, and the site is also convenient to a number of major employers, including the University of Illinois at Chicago, the Illinois Medical District (including the Rush Presbyterian St. Luke Medical Center), the Chicago Technology Park, and the new United Center stadium complex. An excellent private school serves the area, and the public school district recently began a program to improve local public schools.

The city of Chicago has made substantial investments in infrastructure to support the planned development, including water, sewer, and road improvements. The city is also making investments in the roadways just to the north of Homan Square, to define and enhance those neighborhoods, and has targeted Roosevelt

Road and Kedzie Avenue for commercial revitalization. In addition, the city is providing grants for external improvements to homes in adjoining neighborhoods, and nonprofit groups are offering rehabilitation loans. Neighborhood block clubs have formed to help promote community security. Private investment in the area is also planned.

## Project Planning

In 1904, Sears, Roebuck & Company built its headquarters on a 55-acre site in North Lawndale, where it eventually employed 15,000 people. The company began moving employees to its new downtown headquarters in 1974, and by the late 1980s, the 12-block site had been abandoned.

Wanting to leave behind a positive image and legacy, Sears began discussions with The Shaw Company, which had an impressive track record of successful residential development in inner-city neighborhoods, to redevelop the site in a manner that would be a source of pride to the city and the neighborhood. In 1991, Sears and The Shaw Company formed a nonprofit development partnership—West Side Affordable Housing, Inc.—to transform the abandoned Sears complex into a mixed-income community. Because Sears had maintained the buildings in good condition, the structures presented an opportunity to generate jobs and services as well as housing.

Sears deeded all of the residential property to the development partnership. In addi-

tion, two small parcels on the site's northern border were acquired from the city. The partnership gave two and one-half acres of land within the site to the Chicago Park District for a community park. Sears created the Homan Arthington Foundation to be the owner of the commercial property, and the Homan Square Management Company was formed to lease, manage, and develop all of the residential and commercial properties.

The city approved the project as a planned-unit development (PUD), which gave the development partnership the needed flexibility and the city the ability to renegotiate the project with the developer as measurable milestones (such as number of units constructed) were achieved.

Unknown to Sears, the catalog building, power plant, administration building, testing laboratory, and tower had been designated National Historic Landmarks. As a result, the development partnership had to comply with the requirements of Section 106 of the National Environmental Policy Act. Negotiating the teardown of the catalog plant took 13 months. The partnership affirmed its commitment to preserve the remaining buildings, however, and agreed to rehabilitate the exterior of the tower, consistent with Department of the Interior standards. In addition, soil decontamination was required for Phase I and Phase II.

When work on Homan Square began, the site was cleared and vacant except for the five commercial buildings that would be renovated, a parking garage, the original Sears Tower, and the catalog building (which was later demolished). At the time the site was developed, none of the property housed neighborhood residents, so displacement was not an issue.

## Residential Development

The site plan for Homan Square connects the new residential development to the improvements taking place to the north of the site. To strengthen this connection, project construction began at the northern border of the site.

Housing units include single-family houses, townhouses, rowhouses, and flats. Though all home designs are intended to be compatible in scale, architecture, and coloration with the surrounding community, variety in design was sought to avoid an identifiable "project" look and to enable the development to flow visually into the surrounding community. To ensure different product designs, The Shaw Company engaged a different design firm to plan each phase of construction.

Residential development has progressed block by block, according to the financing available and to the partnership's perception of the viability of the market. Sears agreed to provide $30 million in resources during the first five years, including a subsidy for each home built in the project's first two phases. The first phase, which was completed in March 1995, includes 24 detached houses and 50 rental units consisting of 20 townhouses and five buildings of six flats each. All have been sold or leased and are now occupied. The city invested nearly $1.5 million in sewers, streets, and sidewalks for the first phase of the development.

For-sale homes were subsidized through a $20,000-per-home, forgivable loan from the city's New Homes for Chicago program and through the Sears subsidy, which was also forgivable. The city also has a down-payment assistance program that can be used by income-eligible buyers to pay bank-related closing costs. In addition, the federal Mortgage Credit Certificate Program provides eligible buyers with up to $2,000 per year in tax credits.

The development strategy was to create, in Phase I, a market for new housing in this location and to attract a critical mass of residents to give the project momentum. The subsidies made the for-sale homes a terrific value and attracted buyers. But the city places a limit of 24 units on the number of single-family houses it subsidizes in any one development in any one year. Because it wanted to offer a larger number of units to a mixed-income population in the first phase, the development partnership also built subsidized rental housing using federal low-income housing tax credits (LIHTCs). Initial rents were well below the market rate: $395 per month for a two-bedroom unit, compared with the typical $550 to $650 for a two-bedroom unit in an older building; and $490 for a three-bedroom townhouse. Over the long term, the goal has been to enable tenants in the rental housing to own their own units as subsidies for rental units—and the conditions attached to those subsidies—are phased out.

Phase II is under construction. It consists of 24 subsidized single-family houses, eight buildings of subsidized two-family units (16 units); and 16 market-rate, single-family houses. Phase III will contain 72 units, of which 58 will be available at market rates. All housing will be built using a conventional construction loan. Homes in Phase IV will also be unsubsidized. Home prices in the last two phases will be between the home prices in Phase I and those of Phase II. In all, approximately 600 housing units will be built at Homan Square.

The Shaw Company acts as a fee-based developer. Sears receives no financial benefit other than not having to hold, maintain, and pay taxes on the property at some point.

## Commercial Development

All of the remaining commercial buildings will be renovated as needed and either sold or leased. The catalog building, except for the original Sears Tower, has been demolished and will be replaced by housing and a community center. Occupants of the commercial buildings will include private businesses, light industry, public agencies, social service organizations, and promoters of activities to increase the skills and job opportunities of area residents.

Planned community services, which will be offered by various public and private groups, include financial counseling, job readiness training, business startup assistance, health care, family services, adult and child education, fitness programs, and daycare. The community center will also include meeting space for community use.

## Marketing and Management

During the first three months of Phase I, a special effort was made to market the homes first to North Lawndale residents through flyers, brochures, and presentations at meetings. Then the project was advertised to the general public.

The mixed-income nature of the community has not been a marketing issue, but homebuyers initially expressed concern about the nature of the renters. Community members were reassured by the fact that all renters would go through a screening process that included a credit check, a review of their financial statements, a home visit, and security checks. All buyers must participate in homeownership counseling.

Three-quarters of the home purchasers are first-time buyers. Nearly 90 percent of homebuyers so far are from the city of Chicago, and three-fourths are from North Lawndale and nearby communities.

The subsidized homes in Homan Square's first two phases were priced at approximately $100,000 per unit. Unsubsi-

dized units started at $170,000. Phase III homes will be priced between these extremes, at prices that will be affordable to families with incomes between 80 and 120 percent of the median income (in Chicago, from $40,000 to $63,000). Current buyers of the subsidized homes earn $44,000 on average and so are within this income range. The income range for Homan Square residents— renters and buyers—is from $15,000 to $75,000.

Commercial and residential space is marketed and managed by the Homan Square Management Company. Two floors in the administration building have been leased to a variety of tenants, including elected officials, nonprofit organizations, commercial operations, the Rush Primary Care Clinic, the Family Focus Clinic, the Institute for Entrepreneurship, a microlender, and others.

## Experience Gained

- Because one of the project's primary goals was to provide as many homeownership opportunities as possible, accurately determining the market for homeownership was crucial to the project's success.
- Value can be created through sensitive design. In developing Homan Square, a conscious effort was made to maintain open space by preserving existing parks and creating new green spaces

to ensure an appealing environment.

- Development of such an ambitious inner-city infill project requires a partnership involving the city and other public agencies, the community, local nonprofit organizations, conventional lenders, and others. In this case, the key components of the project team included a committed, experienced developer and a patient corporate player who wanted to "do the right thing"; a strong, focused mayor; and an involved community.
- Security has been a primary consideration. During construction, the developer hired security guards. Homes have been clustered in an inverted U design so that public areas are visible from the street. Home security systems, traffic enhancements, fencing, and community policing efforts also reinforce neighborhood security. A major police facility is planned on an adjacent property.
- The project was financially feasible in part because the land was already assembled and was contributed to the development at no cost.
- Large-scale revitalization of inner-city environments takes substantial time and patience. Because development costs will inevitably be higher than anticipated, expenses must be carefully monitored and controlled.

# Homan Square Project Data

## Land Use Information

Site Area: 54.9 acres
Site Area for New Housing and Park: 37.8 acres
Area for Existing Sears Garden: 1.7 acres
Site Area for Commercial/Institutional Uses: 15.4 acres
Total Residential Units: Approximately 600—up to 632 allowed
Total Commercial/Institutional Space: 1 million square feet

## Residential Development Costs

|  | Direct Costs | Indirect Costs | Total Costs[1] |
|---|---|---|---|
| Phase I—Single-family | $105,000 | $25,000 | $130,000 |
| Phase I—Rental | 82,000 | 20,000 | 102,000 |
| Phase II—Single-family (subsidized) | 105,000 | 35,000 | 140,000 |
| Phase II—Single-family (unsubsidized) | 147,000 | 43,000 | 190,000 |

1. Costs refer to costs per unit.

2. Numbers in parentheses refer to numbers of subsidized units.

*Source: ULI Project Reference File report,* Volume 26, Number 11.

## Residential Development Plan

|  | Total Units | For-Sale | Rental |
|---|---|---|---|
| Phase I | 74 (74)[2] | 24 (24) | 50 (50) |
| Phase II | 56 (40) | 56 (40) | – |
| Phase III | 72 (14) | 72 (14) | – |
| Phase IV | To be determined | | |

## Residential Development Funding
## Phases I, II, and III (in $ millions)

| | |
|---|---|
| Private Sources | $31.2 |
|    Sears, Roebuck & Company | 30.0 |
|    LIHTC equity investors | 1.0 |
|    The Shaw Company | 0.2 |
| HUD | 5.2 |
|    HOME funds | 3.6 |
|    CDBG funds | 1.6 |
| City of Chicago | 4.1 |
|    Infrastructure (Phases I and II) | 3.0 |
|    New Homes for Chicago | 1.1 |
| Chicago Park District | 0.5 |
|    Community park | 0.5 |
| Subtotal | $41.0 |
| Individual Home Mortgages | 19.0 |
| Total | $60.0 |

## Chapter Notes

1. Carol Bratley and Barbara Attianese, "Attracting Market-Rate Buyers to Mixed-Income Housing Developments," *Urban Land* (November 1989), p. 24.

2. Having household incomes at or below 60 percent of the area median.

3. Including the East Lake Golf Club and its corporate membership, the Atlanta Housing Authority, the CF Foundation (a charitable foundation established by the Cousins family), Georgia State University, the Atlanta public schools, and the city of Atlanta.

4. From "An Elusive Blend," Part 3 of "Sheltered by Design," *Chicago Tribune* (June 20, 1995), p. 8 of the reprinted series.

5. Ray Gindroz, UDA Architects, Pittsburgh, Pennsylvania, speaking at the HUD Public Housing Summit, May 29, 1996.

6. Telephone interview with Jan Rubin, July 31, 1996.

7. From a memo from Hillary Zimmerman to Diane Suchman, dated September 5, 1996.

## CHAPTER 5

# Public/Private Financing

**T**o attract their intended market, infill housing developments in transitional or distressed inner-city neighborhoods typically must stimulate the market by offering a high-quality housing product at a price that is lower than competing developments in suburban locations. For this goal to be attainable, all infill housing projects need some assistance from the public sector. Projects that include low-income housing must receive sufficient public subsidy to fill the gap between what the housing costs to produce and what the targeted residents can pay.

Because the development of housing on infill sites provides substantial public benefits, developers should expect support and assistance from the local government to overcome the various obstacles to creating successful infill housing—and they must be able to obtain it. Moreover, they should be prepared to suggest specific programs or other kinds of assistance they need from the local government. According to Barry Humphries, president of Renaissance Group, Inc., in Columbus, Ohio, public participation is essential, and the public sector's support is a key early test of feasibility. If public interest is lacking, he cautions, the developer should probably abandon the project.

From the public sector's point of view, investment in infill housing developments in urban neighborhoods is money well spent. Successful residential developments in transitional or declining urban neighborhoods can stimulate additional investment nearby and create momentum

for revitalization of a larger area. For example, since McCormack Baron & Associates began work on the Quality Hill development in Kansas City, Missouri, in1985, the surrounding community has seen a surge of investment. The project has stimulated the development of 800 to 900 additional housing units built by others, plus associated ground-floor retail development in nearby sections of downtown Kansas City. Office developers have also returned to the city: DST/Broadway Square Partners has built (or rehabilitated) a total of more than 1 million additional square feet of office space and parking for approximately 2,800 cars in the downtown since 1989, at a total development cost of about $113 million, generating jobs for some 2,000 people.

This chapter discusses the public/private approach to financing that is usually necessary for infill housing developments. Chapter 6 explores a number of other ways in which the public sector can encourage infill housing development.

A financing problem specific to infill housing development in distressed urban neighborhoods is the fact that because property values tend to be low, the cost of new construction is often higher than the market value of the completed units. If development has involved the rehabilitation of existing structures, the cost could be even higher than that of new development. For example, the developer of Pine Street Cottages estimates that the cost of rehabilitating the existing cottages exceeded the probable cost of new construction by $8,000 to $12,000 per unit. (As noted, however, markets vary. Rehabilitation of a vacant multifamily structure in New York City typically produces a larger, better unit than new construction at a cost 20 to 40 percent lower.[1])

## Public/Private Partnerships

Financing typically involves a number of sources and is achieved through a public/private partnership. Sources and methods of financing vary according to the needs and opportunities presented by the project itself and by available public and private resources. The strategy can include various combinations of private financing, federal programs, and city and state contributions of land, tax abatements, and capital grants. Federal programs include low-income housing tax credits (LIHTCs), historic rehabilitation tax credits, FHA (Federal Housing Administration) Section 202 housing for the elderly, HUD project-based Section 8 monies, and the HUD HOME program. In 1996, HUD began a new program to provide seed money, in the form of grants and loan guarantees, to help create neighborhoods designated as "homeownership zones."

States may help fund infill housing development through loans and grants from the state housing finance agency, proceeds from bond issues, and equity from state low-income or rehabilitation tax credits, as well as a variety of other programs to achieve specific development goals.

Because infill housing projects vary so greatly in concept and execution, flexible funding assistance is most valuable. Local jurisdictions can help finance a project through targeted assistance programs and actions and/or by encouraging investment from the private sector. Cities, through various agencies and authorities, can provide financial assistance by using their own funds from general revenues or other sources, through establishing tax increment financing (TIF) districts, and by issuing bonds. Cities can help developers to obtain financing by providing a loan guarantee or a letter of credit, offering developers city-owned land or swapping key parcels, waiving fees and taxes, and helping to subsidize the retail component of a new mixed-use development until it becomes profitable.

Tax increment financing, an approach by which a portion of additional tax revenue within a designated district is dedicated to financing improvements within that district, has been highly successful in encouraging infill development in some areas. The TIF district strategy reduces land use uncertainty through zoning and design guidelines, transfers infrastructure costs to the public sector, and ensures a high-quality visual environment.

In Dallas, a new upscale community, the State-Thomas neighborhood, was built on 135 acres of mostly undeveloped land and freeway frontage near existing Victorian houses close to the downtown. Through grass-roots advocacy by area residents and property owners, through designation of the State-Thomas planned development district to generate a flexible planning framework, and through city investments in the area funded through tax increment financing, for-profit developers were able to start the new housing projects that became the State-Thomas neighborhood. According to Tom Cole of the Dallas Economic Development Department, the quality of development has been high and has led to additional private investment. In fact, in the State-Thomas TIF district, $6.1 million in public investment has led to $55.4 million in private investment. Even more astounding is the public/private ratio of $1 to $18.7 in Dallas's City Place TIF district, where a $1.7 million public investment has resulted in $32.3 million in private investment.[2]

Private sector debt financing from a traditional institutional investor, such as a bank or savings institution, is a typical component of a financing package. Such investments are encouraged by the requirements of the federal Community Reinvestment Act; nonetheless, the lender will expect a return on its investment. But because development might not have occurred recently in an older urban neighborhood, conventional lenders may view the market there as untested and risky.

Lenders may not be familiar with affordable or mixed-income housing projects or urban neighborhoods. If a project involves a mix of uses, as many infill developments do, comparable projects are often not available. Even if they are, many banks separate residential and commercial lending, which means that no one person will understand the project. In addition, infill projects may be difficult to sell to the secondary market, which tends not to underwrite condominiums, co-ops, mixed-use developments, and other forms of urban housing.[3] Often, the developer's track record, especially with similar kinds of projects, is important in determining whether conventional financing will be available.

Sometimes, the developer has to invent his own solution. Milton Jones, developer of Regal Trace, a 400-unit rental infill development in Fort Laud-

Homes in the Quality Hill development in Kansas City include both apartments and townhomes.

erdale, Florida, helped to create his own private sector lender by working patiently and persistently with the banking community to help form a lending consortium that provided the project's construction and permanent loans.

Fannie Mae (FNMA), Freddie Mac (FHLMC), and the Federal Home Loan Bank (FHLB) have set up various programs to encourage lenders to invest in affordable housing and inner-city neighborhoods. For example, Fannie Mae's American Communities Fund, established in 1996, makes equity investments ranging in size from approximately $1 million to $5 million that are tailored to the needs of affordable housing and related mixed-use, commercial, and retail developments in emerging neighborhoods. FHLB, through its Affordable Housing Program, provides member institutions with direct subsidies and subsidized advances to enable them to make grants or below-market loans to assist in the acquisition, construction, and/or rehabilitation of affordable housing (rental or ownership).

City governments can help attract private investment for infill development projects by using a strategy that includes several elements: working with developers and lenders to structure incentives and restrictions in an effort to match rewards with risks; maintaining consistent, predictable programs and funding over time; developing and

promoting investment products that help satisfy bank Community Reinvestment Act obligations; permitting flexibility in income targeting and affordability ratios; and delegating the underwriting of public/private loan programs to participating lenders of financial institutions that put their own funds at risk.[4] And the city can assist a home-buyer who chooses a house in an infill housing development through, for example, financing assistance, downpayment assistance, or relaxed restrictions on resales.

Other sources of public and private financing may be available for developments that are targeted at low-income or mixed-income households.

# The City of Cleveland's Neighborhood Revitalization Incentives

Every city has a wide range of financial and regulatory resources that can be tapped as direct and indirect incentives to encourage private investment in its inner-city neighborhoods. Public/private partnerships are at the heart of the revitalization efforts taking place in Cleveland's 35 neighborhoods, stimulated by some financial assistance and useful development tools, including the following:

*Community reinvestment by banks.* Since 1991, the city's seven banks, one thrift, and Fannie Mae (FNMA) have committed nearly $1.3 billion in private funds to the city's neighborhoods. Cleveland appears to be the first city in the United States to secure such a large reinvestment commitment from so many banks.

*Focused foundation support.* In 1989, local foundations, civic associations, the corporate community, and the Ford Foundation established Neighborhood Progress, Inc. (NPI), as a local intermediary to escalate investment in and increase resources for community economic development. NPI invests these resources in community-based organizations and large-scale projects that serve as catalysts for revitalizing Cleveland's neighborhoods.

*Low-income housing tax credits.* Despite the recent uncertainty associated with the federal tax credit program, local banks and corporations have embraced the program enthusiastically whenever opportunities to use tax credits have materialized. The National Equity Fund of the Local Initiatives Support Cor-poration (LISC), the nation's largest syndicator of tax credits, has brought nearly $30 million in equity investment to the Cleveland area. The Enterprise Foundation has invested or committed an additional $43 million.

*Housing trust fund.* Cleveland's new housing construction mania has been fueled by the city's housing trust fund. Established in 1991 by the White administration to stimulate the production of affordable housing, the fund offers low-interest loans that have been the targets of heated competition among prospective developers. The fund is financed with federal Community Development Block Grant (CDBG) and HOME monies. Over the past five years, the city's commitment of $21.3 million has leveraged well over $100 million in private investment and thus has facilitated the construction of 1,656 dwelling units and the rehabilitation of an additional 1,308 units.

*Neighborhood development bond funds.* The city's neighborhood development bond program is used to finance capital improvements that stimulate new housing construction. At least $1 million a year is raised from the sale of general obligation bonds to investors on the open market. The proceeds have been targeted for site acquisition, site preparation, and infrastructure improvements for 15 subdivisions.

*Neighborhood development investment funds.* In 1994, the city established a locally funded, $40 million revolving loan program to stimulate the creation and retention of neighborhood-based jobs. Of the initial funding, $10 million has been set aside for the development of new housing. Neighborhood investment funds must be invested outside the downtown business district.

*Electricity discounts.* Cleveland Public Power is a municipally owned utility. It grants residential and commercial customers a savings of approximately 30 percent on monthly electric bills, compared with its competitor's rates. Lower-cost electricity is an important marketing tool for housing and economic development in the city.

*Low-cost land.* The city holds approximately 6,000 parcels in its land bank—mostly formerly tax-delinquent properties. Cleveland sells buildable vacant lots for $100 to persons or businesses demonstrating a commitment to build. It also makes nonbuildable lots available for $1 to adjacent homeowners for yard expansion, gardens, or garages.

*Tax abatement.* Liberalization of the city's property tax abatement policy in 1990 has been instrumental in facilitating residential, commercial, and industrial development. The abatement period for newly constructed housing is ten years; for developments of 25 or more units, it is 15 years.

*Source:* Diane Corcelli and Victor Dubina, "Cleveland's Rejuvenated Neighborhoods," *Urban Land* (April 1996), p. 50.

Depending upon the location of the project, the project type, the target market, and the nature of the development partnership, these sources might include, for instance, public and private pension funds, housing trust funds, corporations, foundations, other charitable organizations, and intermediaries such as the Enterprise Foundation, Local Initiatives Support Corporation (LISC), and National Housing Services (NHS).

The typical infill housing development located in a transitional or distressed city neighborhood will require financing that is pieced together with individual financing streams from a number of sources, each of which has its own agenda and requirements. It is not unusual for projects to require seven or eight sources of financing. Infill housing projects tend to be unique responses to individual circumstances and opportunities, and the kinds and amounts of financing available will vary from project to project and location to location. Thus, there is no replicable model or system for financing these kinds of developments.

According to John McIlwain, president of the Fannie Mae Foundation, first-mortgage debt financing can usually be obtained from conventional lenders (though often for only 70 to 80 percent of a project's cost). Predevelopment funds, however, generally must come from the developer or, in the case of partnerships that involve nonprofits, foundations. And many developers need to obtain gap financing to cover the period between completion of construction and lease-up.

Because different developers tend to specialize in certain types of projects, they tend to rely repeatedly on certain types of financing or public sector participation. In developing mixed-income projects in or near central cities, McCormack Baron & Associates has found that it can attract financial resources to urban redevelopment projects that are sufficiently large to improve the neighborhood image, and that local foundations can be a source of significant financing for central-city development that has a social purpose.

Richard Baron notes that, to make his company's projects work financially, he looks for public improvements; land acquisition, site preparation, and environmental remediation by the city; tax abatements or tax increment financing; and possibly additional soft financing from state housing finance agencies (HFAs) or passed-through HUD Community Development Block Grant (CDBG) or HOME funds. Though many believe that LIHTCs are difficult to use for mixed-income housing, Baron's firm typically relies on low-

income housing tax credits—combined, where appropriate, with historic rehabilitation tax credits—for project equity in financing mixed-income developments.

The Corcoran Jennison Companies typically uses funds from tax-exempt bonds issued through states, counties, and cities, as well as from HUD Section 8 project-based subsidies and certificates. In addition, the firm looks for special tax deals, such as property tax abatements.

Because the federal low-income housing tax credits and tax-exempt financing are among the most frequently used sources of funds for developing infill rental housing, their use is described briefly in the next section of this chapter.

## The Federal Low-Income Housing Tax Credit[5]

The federal low-income housing tax credit (LIHTC), enacted in 1986 as Section 42 of the IRS Code and made permanent in 1993, is the most important public financial incentive program spurring low-income rental housing development within and outside of central cities. It now finances about 100,000 housing units each year—35 percent of all newly constructed rental units nationally and 94 percent of all new or rehabilitated rental apartments for low-income households (see Figure 1, next page). Because it offers investors a tax credit for money invested in low-income housing, the LIHTC represents a shift away from rental subsidy and loan guarantee programs that have required annual budget appropriations. In this respect, it resembles the form of federal subsidy used to promote the production of owner-occupied housing.

Although the tax credit program can be cumbersome and baffling for developers, it offers many advantages. The tax credit can typically provide the financing for a development. Many investors require significant guarantees from developers but will commit to and fund a project before it is fully leased, which is not the case with market-rate multifamily developments. Because most investors are seeking credits, often the developer as the general partner can benefit from the residual cash flow.

Increased competition for tax credits has pushed the cost per credit up three to five cents in the last year, which has enabled developers to build high-quality housing similar to market-rate properties, compared with the cost-controlled HUD-subsidized housing of the 1960s and 1970s.

Tax credits allow developers to obtain significant equity, reducing the size of the mortgage, which can translate into rents as much as 10 to 20 percent below market. Generally, tax-credit properties rent sooner and stay filled longer than their sister, market-rate properties.

The credit essentially is an equity incentive vehicle, as well as, in one small respect, a debt-enhancement vehicle. The credit is large and secure enough that it leverages private investor equity, which accounts for as much as 50 to 60 percent of the total development cost for newly constructed properties.

To obtain the credit, a developer applies to an allocating agency, usually the state housing finance authority, for a share of the state's credits. Developers raise equity by selling, either directly or through a middle agent or syndicator, ownership interests in properties. Currently, equity interests are being sold at 55 to 75 cents per credit dollar. (Investors price their equity close to the present value of the ten-year stream of credits.) Typically, the developer retains an ownership interest in the property as a general partner and guarantees investment performance, including the flow of credits.

Each state receives an annual allocation of tax credits that represents $1.25 per capita. States can also receive additional credits through a reallocation of a national pool of unused credits at the end of the year. Credits for properties financed with federally tax-exempt mortgage revenue bonds come from a separate pool. In recent years, almost all states have fully allocated their credits, and many states have extremely competitive allocating environments, receiving applications for three to five times the credit available.

All credits must be allocated in accordance with the states' qualified allocation plans (QAPs), which define the priorities and competitive criteria for awarding the credits. Most states give preference to projects serving the lowest-income residents and having the longest duration of rent and income controls. Other selection considerations include project location, housing needs characteristics, development characteristics, participation of local nonprofit organizations, special-needs populations, and the length of waiting lists for public housing. States typically use a scoring system to rank applicants requesting allocations.

The IRS requires that each state set aside a minimum of 10 percent of its allocation to developments involving a nonprofit organization as an equity owner that materially participates in the development and operation of the property for at least 15 years. If the nonprofit should fail and be replaced, it must be replaced by another nonprofit. For these and other reasons related to the technical and financial capacity of nonprofit housing providers, as well as the stringent definition of "materially participate," use of the 10 percent set-aside has had mixed results. Many developers team up with nonprofits or municipalities but apply for the general set-aside of tax credits, by-passing the material participation requirements.

## Figure 1. Sources of Funds: Multifamily New Construction

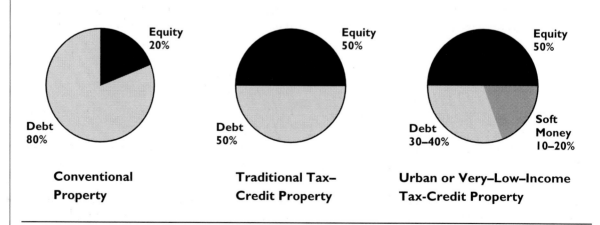

Source: Susan Hobart and Robert Schwartz, *Financing Multifamily Housing Using Section 42 Low-Income Housing Tax Credits,* ULI Working Paper #654, August 1996, p. 5.

## Figuring the Credit

The amount of credit allocated to each property is determined by a formula laid out in the authorizing legislation:

> Eligible Development Cost Basis x Applicable Fraction (percent of units meeting Section 42 rent/income rules) x Credit Rate (either 4 percent or 9 percent, depending on type of property and debt financing) = Annual Tax Credit

Costs allowed in establishing the eligible credit basis include costs of construction or rehabilitation and may include "soft" costs, such as architectural, engineering, and development fees. Soft costs related to permanent debt (e.g., origination fees, closing costs) and equity financing are not eligible. Because land costs are not depreciable, they are excluded from the eligible basis. The inclusion of landscaping, impact fees, and off-site improvements—though these are often eligible— is determined by the particular facts, usually after consulting with a tax attorney or accountant.

New construction or substantial rehabilitation expenses not financed by a federal source receive a 9 percent annual credit. For rehabilitation properties involving acquisition, a 4 percent annual credit is given on the eligible costs of acquisition. The actual credit percentages vary monthly and are indexed to ten-year U.S. Treasury bond yields.

For projects that use federally tax-exempt debt, such as mortgage revenue bonds, to finance 50 percent or more of their total cost, only the 4 percent credit is given. Projects using federal tax-exempt bonds are also subject to different credit allocation rules.

For any tax-credit-eligible project that is located in a "difficult-to-develop" area, as defined by HUD, the qualified basis upon which the credit is calculated can be increased by 30 percent.

Grants or below-market-rate federal loans used to pay for development costs generally are subtracted from the eligible basis, thus lowering the credit amount. Loans funded through local or state awards of Community Development Block Grants, however, do not reduce the eligible basis. Other low-interest loan programs, such as the federal HOME program of the Federal Home Loan Bank Board's Affordable Housing Program, have particular rules for classification when used with the credit.

To prevent developers from capitalizing excess development fees by leveraging more debt and equity than needed, the IRS requires that the amount of credit allocated not exceed the amount needed to make the property financially feasible.

At least 20 percent of the units must be set aside for households making 50 percent or less of the area median gross income (AMGI), or 40 percent of the units must be set aside for households at 60 percent or less of the AMGI. Some tax credit allocators (such as New York City and Chicago) have special set-asides. Owners must agree to comply with income restrictions for at least 15 years. Because rents are based on a percentage of area median incomes rather than tenants' actual incomes, rents paid by tenants can exceed 30 percent of their incomes.

Throughout the country, LIHTCs have enabled states to encourage the development of housing for households with very low incomes, to target difficult-to-reach populations, and to provide new housing in underserved areas. When combined with other sources of capital, these tax credits can be used to promote neighborhood revitalization strategies in inner-city neighborhoods.

## Using LIHTCs with Historic Tax Credits

In addition to spurring the development of low-income housing, LIHTCs, alone or in combination with historic rehabilitation tax credits (HRTCs), often provide the source of equity financing that makes a mixed-income project work. Combining the credits generates more equity because of the greater total tax benefits. The rehabilitation tax credit equals 20 percent of "qualified rehabilitation expenditures" spent on a certified historic structure that is subject to depreciation.

Buildings listed on the National Register of Historic Places or located within a registered historic district are eligible for federal historic rehabilitation tax credits, so long as the rehabilitation meets the Secretary of the Interior's *Standards for Rehabilitation*. The standards apply to the interiors and exteriors of all types of historic buildings, landscape features, and the buildings' sites and environments, with the goal of preserving the buildings' character-defining features, spaces, and materials.[6] In 1993, almost one-third of the housing units that were rehabilitated using the historic rehabilitation tax credit also relied on the LIHTC.

When a developer uses both the LIHTC and the rehabilitation tax credit, the eligible basis for the LIHTC must be reduced by the amount of the rehabilitation tax credit. In most cases, the historic credits leverage additional investor equity, which is then used to cover the extraordinary rehabilitation costs that historic buildings typically require. An investor can claim the historic credits for the first year that the property is placed in service.

For example, McCormack Baron & Associates has completed the first phase of Ninth Square, a mixed-use development near Yale University in the historic district of New Haven, Connecticut, in partnership with The Related Companies, LP, of New York City. Ninth Square's first phase involves a total of 335 residential units, 50,000 net square feet of ground-floor retail/commercial space, two parking decks, landscaped interior courtyards and walkways, and extensive public improvements on four city blocks. Financing sources for Phase I have totaled $86.6 million and are composed of the following:

- Taxable bonds purchased by Yale from the Connecticut Housing Finance Authority: $10 million.
- Tax-exempt bonds issued by CHFA: $31.8 million.
- City special obligation bonds (repaid from increments in the property tax receipts of the benefiting area): $9.5 million.
- City loan and grant money: $4.6 million.
- Former state departments of housing and economic development: $7 million.
- Urban Development Action Grant funds from HUD: $8.9 million.
- Equity raised through the sale of historic rehabilitation tax credits, in combination with the sale of low-income housing tax credits: $14.8 million.

The developer's use of the LIHTC carries the requirement that 58 percent of the apartments in the first phase be rented to qualifying low-income households.

Another example, Mercy Family Plaza, an award-winning affordable housing project developed by the for-profit Ibex Group in San Francisco, involved the historic rehabilitation of four significant buildings of a former hospital complex, as described in a project profile in Chapter 3. The project obtained $1 million in HRTCs and $3.4 million in LIHTCs, for project equity. Fannie Mae, as the project's only limited partner, purchased the tax credits. The development's total cost was $6.25 million.

Project funding for Mercy Family Plaza was typically complicated, including a grant from Markborough California Properties through San Francisco's Affordable Housing Fund; a grant from the state of California; two short-term, below-market loans, one from the Catherine McAuley Housing Foundation and one from the Low-Income Housing Foundation; and a long-term, below-market purchase-money note from the buildings' previous owner, Mercy Services Corporation, with which to purchase the buildings.

Mercy Services Corporation retains the ownership of the land, leasing it to Mercy Charities Housing, the project's owner, for 99 years. The lease includes a permanent deed restriction limiting the use of the site to affordable, income-restricted housing, which has reduced the value of the site. Under the terms of the ground lease, the payments on the property have been deferred until the project's ninth or tenth year.

Construction financing was obtained from Union Bank, and permanent financing came from Savings Association Mortgage Company (SAMCO), a nonprofit consortium of thrifts that finances affordable housing development.[7]

## Tax-Exempt Bonds

Many infill housing developments, and especially those targeted at mixed-income populations, rely heavily on tax-exempt bond financing. Boston developer Joseph Corcoran explains that the key advantage of tax-exempt bond money is that it carries an interest rate 2.5 points lower than market-rate loans and, when HUD-insured or when insured by a state housing finance agency, like California's, it has a 40-year instead of a 25-year term. This enables Corcoran to build with lower-cost money. In addition, he obtains more subsidies for the lower-income units. The debt service is lower than it would be for a straight market-rate deal because even the market-rate units benefit from the bond financing's lower interest rate and longer term. Such a cost advantage makes it possible for the developer to build in more quality and to make the project more competitive.

Under federal law, tax-exempt revenue bonds can be issued by state or local governments to help finance the development of low-income multifamily housing. Issuers sell bonds to investors whose income from such investments is exempt from federal—and, in most cases, state—income taxes. Consequently, issuers can market bonds at lower-than-conventional interest rates. Issuers usually seek a bond rating from one of

Summerfield Apartments is a 52-unit, affordable housing development in Charlotte, North Carolina, that was developed by Crosland Properties and the Charlotte-Mecklenburg Housing Partnership using low-income housing tax credits. The project features distinctive contemporary architecture.

A new three-unit townhouse built as part of the Summit Place development in St. Paul, Minnesota, was designed to complement the architectural traditions of the neighborhood.

the rating agencies, such as Standard & Poor's or Moody's, whose rating further reduces the interest rate payable on the debt. Revenue bonds are not guaranteed by the issuing agency; they rely on project cash flow to pay bondholders. Therefore, issuers often use some form of credit enhancement, such as a letter of credit or bond insurance, to obtain a top rating from the rating agencies and thus to provide liquidity for variable-rate debt. A letter of credit gives the bonds the same rating as the bank issuing the letter.

Use of tax-exempt bonds imposes income restrictions for the term of the bonds. Typically, 20 percent of the housing units must be affordable by households making up to 50 percent of the area median income, or 40 percent of the units must be affordable to households making up to 60 percent of the area median income.

It is important to note that projects financed with tax-exempt bonds that use low-income housing tax credits are not subject to the volume cap for 9 percent tax credits. Instead, tax-exempt financing is subject to its own cap, called the "private activity volume cap." Projects receiving subsidized financing, including low-income units financed with tax-exempt bonds, can receive the 4 percent LIHTC but are not eligible for the 9 percent credit.

According to Tom Safran, the availability of 4 percent LIHTCs for projects financed with tax-exempt bonds is often the key that enables these projects to go forward. He notes that in California, as elsewhere, competition for 9 percent LIHTCs is stiff. In 1996, for example, only one in five projects seeking 9 percent LIHTCs from the state of California received them. In 1997, the state held a lottery to determine which of the many applicant projects would get the 9 percent credits.

But projects financed through tax-exempt bonds can get 4 percent LIHTCs by right. Unable to obtain 9 percent LIHTCs for two of his projects in 1996, Tom Safran reworked their financing, applied for tax-exempt funding, and obtained 4 percent LIHTCs—thereby salvaging the projects and the $4.3 million and $8.4 million in local money that had been committed to them. The secret of this strategy, Safran adds, is to apply for tax-exempt financing early in the year, before the private activity volume cap has been reached.

Under the Tax Reform Act of 1986, public agencies may issue a tax-exempt bond if a Section 501c(3) tax-exempt entity uses the proceeds for its exempt purposes and complies with other restrictions. Such an organization can use the bond proceeds to develop or acquire housing that it will own. The bonds are not subject to the cap on volume applicable to agency-issued multifamily bonds. Each Section 501c(3) organization can use up to $150 million in bonds issued for housing on its behalf.

These bonds tend to sell at an interest rate that is about 25 basis points lower than that of other tax-exempt bonds, as interest on the bonds is not a tax preference subject to the alternative minimum tax. One potential disadvantage of these bonds however, is that the nonprofit entity cannot form a limited partnership to syndicate the project and to sell low-income housing tax credits to investors. Syndication would violate the rule that requires the benefiting project to be owned by a Section 501c(3) organization.

## Putting the Pieces Together

The fragmented nature of today's complex financing and the restrictions on the use of funds from each source can make it difficult to finance large or comprehensive developments. The following examples illustrate the variety of public/private financing strategies that have been used for infill housing developments in various parts of the United States:

- In Atlanta, Ackerman & Company was able to offer condominiums at Siena at Renaissance Park—52 walkup units in three buildings on a 2.7-acre urban infill site—at monthly payments that were lower than the rents for comparable area apartments. A tax exemption gained through the state Residential Urban Enterprise Act eliminated for five years all property taxes (except bonded indebtedness and sanitation charges) in city-designated zones. Property taxes are phased in during the next five years.

  The program saved buyers $120 to $200 per month during the first five years. The city's Urban Residential Finance Authority provided mortgage funds to buyers through a tax-exempt bond issue at 30-year fixed rates of 8.9 percent, with a 2-to-1 buydown available at a starting rate of 6.9 percent. The developer paid 4.7 points toward acquisition and obtained the commitment for financing from a local company.

- In Minneapolis, Brighton Development Corporation, in partnership with Central Community Housing Trust (a nonprofit corporation), purchased five old buildings—three of which were in a historic district—and renovated the units as Elliot Park West. Of the 218 units, 30 percent are single-room-occupancy (SRO) units; the remainder are more typical low-income rentals. The Greater Minneapolis Metropolitan Housing Corporation provided seed money for predevelopment, and rehabilitation financing was obtained from the syndication of low-income housing tax credits and historic tax credits.

  The first mortgage, from the Minnesota Housing Finance Agency, came from the

sale of tax-exempt housing revenue bonds. The city provided "soft seconds" from three sources: the Minneapolis Community Development Agency, which provided a long-term nonamortizing loan; a city fund designated for the replacement of SROs that had been demolished for the construction of a convention center; and contributions to the city made by another developer in exchange for other assistance.

- The Milwaukee Department of City Development, working through a nonprofit affiliate, is developing CityHomes, a middle-income, single-family, for-sale subdivision of 40 to 50 houses on a two-block parcel near 20th and Walnut streets. The units will be constructed by Trustway Builders, a for-profit company. The cost of construction will exceed the value of the completed units, and most of the difference will be funded through tax increment financing. The city is approaching private corporations and philanthropic organizations for funds to make up the difference. No federal funds will be used, to avoid the need to comply with costly federal regulations. The city will also pay for infrastructure, site preparation, and miscellaneous costs like security, marketing, and sales.

- In Pittsburgh, the mixed-income, mixed rental/for-sale Crawford Square development was financed through public funds from city and state governments, conventional mortgage debt, foundation loans and grants, and equity from the private sector. For the first phase of development, which consisted of rental housing, the first mortgage came from a consortium of local banks, the second from the Pennsylvania Housing and Finance Agency, the third from a consortium of Pittsburgh-based foundations, the fourth from the Pennsylvania Department of Community Affairs, and the fifth and sixth from the Urban Redevelopment Authority of Pittsburgh. Equity capital came from local and national corporations through the syndication of low-income housing tax credits. In addition, Pittsburgh provided almost $12 million in infrastructure improvements. The financing mix was different for subsequent phases and for the for-sale houses.

  According to McCormack Baron & Associates, development coordinator for the project, each participant was necessary to the deal and supplied an element of credibility that convinced the others to become involved.

- In Los Angeles, a historic building was saved and 124 units of housing were built near a subway station when the Metropolitan Transportation Authority (MTA) and the Community Redevelopment Agency (CRA) worked with private developers on the Grand Central Market project, which also includes office and retail space.

Originally, the developer could not get financing for the residential portion of the project, so the redevelopment agency stepped in and issued bonds totaling $44 million to finance the project. Both multifamily housing bonds and redevelopment bonds were used for the restoration of the historically significant commercial portion of the project.

The MTA, along with the redevelopment agency, played a critical role in project financing by making direct payments of debt service for the bonds. The two agencies are being reimbursed through project income and bond proceeds.

## The Developer's Return

Though there is much satisfaction in helping to revitalize a distressed urban neighborhood, developers of infill housing projects are in business to make a profit. Often, the developer's profit comes from fees paid by the development partnership for the various services the developer provides. Depending on the firm and the project, these services might include certain predevelopment studies, managing the development process, marketing the for-sale units, or managing the rental units. A development firm that packages financing for projects might also receive a separate fee for that service, as well as syndication fees for the LIHTCs.

In developing infill housing projects, Shaw Homes of Chicago typically receives fees for the predevelopment work, such as creating a master plan, obtaining entitlements for the project, preparing financial models, and designing a marketing plan. In addition, the firm earns fees for developing the project and for marketing for-sale homes (or, if a rental project, for managing the property). Typically, fees for development and construction average 6 to 8 percent of project revenues. For a rental project, the typical development fee is 7 to 10 percent of total development cost; the management fee is in the 6 percent range. For example, in the Homan Square project, the corporate sponsor paid a planning retainer that funded the use of staff time until project planning and negotiations had been completed. In addition, the firm earns a development fee amounting to 3 percent of sales and a construction fee from the sale of for-sale homes. The marketing fee is contingent on a home's actual sale and equals 4 percent of the home's selling price.

McCormack Baron & Associates of St. Louis is also a fee developer. According to Richard Baron, the firm typically charges a 10 percent developer fee that is paid out over a five-year period. Management fees stabilize the peaks and valleys of the development business. The firm has wrestled with the issue of how to cover its predevelopment costs. Before 1989, it had a working line of credit. When the recession hit, however, banks became severely regulated, and deals became more difficult and time-consuming to structure. As a result, McCormack Baron has redirected its approach and now asks the local community to provide predevelopment money, generally through block grants or federal program funds. In addition, the firm has tapped foundations for unsecured loans that are repaid at the time of closing.

According to Tom Safran, each project is different and presents different opportunities. His firm, Thomas Safran & Associates (TSA), retains ownership of every project it develops and makes money through development fees, a percentage of the project's cash flow, management fees, and an increase in value as a result of project appreciation. In California, development fees are limited to the lower of either $1.2 million per project or 15 percent of the "eligible basis" for obtaining LIHTCs (which is essentially total project costs minus land and certain fees).

When practicable, Safran has developed projects that are the optimum size to increase management efficiency and to maximize developer fees—typically about 100 units. TSA's projects are sometimes developed in partnership with nonprofit organizations that can obtain preferential loan terms and property tax dispensations.

The management fees that TSA earns for project oversight and management are controlled by project lenders. These fees vary but are typically in the range of 4 to 8 percent of gross operating income. Recently, TSA has begun exploring the potential for outsourcing selected management functions to take advantage of greater efficiencies and profit potential.

# Wells Court Apartments, Atlanta, Georgia

Use of LIHTCs made possible the development of the Wells Court Commons apartments.

Wells Court Commons is located in metropolitan Atlanta, in a community that has a mix of owner-occupied housing and multifamily housing built during Atlanta's last boom in the late 1970s. Located at 1856 Wells Drive in the southwestern section of the city, it was an existing development with 62 two-bedroom/one-bath units and five two-story buildings. Each unit has 850 square feet of living space.

The property had been vacant and boarded up for several years. The rehabilitated units were marketed to small families, with seven units targeted to people with disabilities and four to families from the public housing waiting list. The developer has significant experience in developing housing in transitional urban neighborhoods and, in particular, in converting boarded-up buildings.

The 4.5-acre, rectangular site lies in an established neighborhood, close to services, but many of the area's multifamily buildings are in various stages of transition from newly renovated to boarded-up and abandoned. The Resolution Trust Corporation (RTC) held title to Wells Court and, in September 1993, sold it under its affordable housing program. The property is subject to a land use restriction agreement, which will remain in effect for 40 years. The agreement requires the owner

When work began on Wells Court in Atlanta, the property consisted of 62 vacant units in five ramshackle, two-story buildings. The rehabilitation effort included road repaving and extensive landscaping.

to make available at least 20 units for occupancy by low-income families, i.e., those with incomes below 80 percent of median income. Rents are correspondingly restricted to 30 percent of the applicable income limit and are computed as under the tax credit program, with rents ranging from $220 to $425 per month, excluding utilities.

Because the property has used HOME funds, it has been subject to HOME's programmatic requirements as well, enforced through a restriction agreement. Under the HOME program, at least 40 percent of the units must be restricted to very-low-income residents, a greater number than provided for through either the affordable housing or the tax credit program. In addition, rent cannot exceed 30 percent of the applicable income limit of the Section 8 fair market rent.

Built in 1971, the buildings are wood-frame with brick exteriors, new roofs, and new gutters and downspouts. New, insulated windows and exterior doors have been installed. The developer replaced the HVAC

and water heaters with energy-efficient systems and individual gas meters, Sheetrocked and painted all walls, put in new floor coverings, and, in many cases, installed new bathroom fixtures. Five percent of the units were made wheelchair-accessible. The community includes a laundry building, a new 2,000-square-foot community building, play and picnic grounds, a small pool, and improved fencing, security lighting, and landscaping. The developer and property manager worked with the local YMCA to provide after-school child care services in the new community building for the low-income working families.

Because of the multiple rent and household restrictions, a creative marketing program was undertaken to qualify not only people with very low incomes but also those who are able to pay the rent themselves. The units leased faster than had been projected, and the development was 100 percent occupied when the last unit was placed in service.

The credit cost for Wells Court was more than 58 cents

on the dollar, with all units qualifying for the LIHTC. The key to making this development affordable, with its more than $3 million development costs, was obtaining a $1 million, 1 percent interest-rate home loan from the state of Georgia and a $250,000 1 percent interest-rate loan from the city of Atlanta. Both loans are amortized over 30 years, with accruing and deferring interest. Both the city and the state have agreed to subordinate their loans to the conventional lender.

Despite the nearly $50,000-per-unit development cost, the HOME money at the 1 percent interest and the tax-credit equity infusion allowed for a minimal first mortgage, which permitted the developer to schedule a $2,800-per-year/per-unit operating expense budget and still keep rents within the range of $220 to $425 monthly.

*Source:* Susan Hobart and Robert Schwartz, *Financing Multifamily Housing Using Section 42 Low-Income Housing Tax Credits,* ULI Working Paper 654 (August 1996).

# Strathern Park, Sun Valley, Los Angeles, California

The Strathern Park development illustrates the multilayered financing required to produce high-quality, low-income housing.

Strathern Park is a 241-unit, rental apartment development on an 8.68-acre site in the largely Latino Sun Valley section of Los Angeles. The project, which was completed in 1991, won a ULI Award for Excellence in 1995. Three-quarters of the units are targeted to families earning less than 50 percent of the area median income, the remainder to families who earn less than 60 percent of the area median. Strathern Park was fully leased at the completion of construction, with more than 3,000 families applying. It still has a waiting list today.

The project consists of eight-unit and 16-unit clusters of extensively landscaped, two-story walkup buildings, so that there are no interior corridors. Amenities include a recreation building, three tot lots, and landscaped courtyards. Laundries, barbecues, and seating are located next to children's play grounds. Each unit has a private patio or balcony. Sections of concrete parking lots have been designed to be roped off for basketball and skateboarding. Buildings are oriented to

Strathern Park, a 241-unit apartment development targeted at low- and very-low-income households in Sun Valley, California, was planned to include private open space for each unit.

## Summary of Project Financing

|  | Millions of Dollars |
| --- | --- |
| **Preconstruction Financing** | |
| Seed capital from the developer, TSA | $2.0 |
| Land acquisition loan from the CRA | 4.3 |
|  | $6.3 |
| **Construction Financing** | |
| Partial equity from tax credit investor | $3.9 |
| Permanent gap loan from the CRA | 6.3 |
| HUD HoDAG loan | 5.2 |
| Wells Fargo construction loan | 7.8 |
|  | $23.2 |
| **Permanent Financing** | |
| Equity from tax credit investor | $7.8 |
| Permanent gap loan from the CRA | 6.3 |
| HUD HoDAG | 5.2 |
| CCRC permanent loan | 6.2 |
|  | $25.5 |

promote the security of streets and common areas, and the entire site is gated to control access.

Financing the $25.5 million project required seven funding sources with per-unit costs totaling $106,000. Thomas Safran & Associates (TSA), the project developer, funded predevelopment costs (architecture, engineering, legal fees, and so forth). The city of Los Angeles's Community Redevelopment Agency (CRA) provided a $4.3 million land acquisition loan. Wells Fargo Bank loaned the developer $7.8 million to build the project. Once construction financing was in place, the CRA's land loan was taken out by a $5.2 million HUD loan through the Housing Development Action Grant (HoDAG) program. The HoDAG loan was administered jointly by the CRA and the city of Los Angeles Housing Preservation and Production Department. At the same time, the CRA funded a long-term gap loan of $6.3 million, to be disbursed along with the conventional construction loan.

During the predevelopment stage of the project, TSA received an allocation of federal low-income housing tax credits from the state. These credits had been syndicated through the Boston Financial Group, bringing a total of $7.8 million in equity investment to the project. A portion of this capital was made available to the project at the start of construction, and the remaining amounts were contributed to the project upon completion of construction, upon permanent loan funding, and after a period of stabilized occupancy.

When the project had been completed, the construction loan was taken out by a combination of investor equity and a long-term, $6.2 million first-trust deed loan from the California Community Reinvestment Corporation (CCRC). The $5.2 million HoDAG loan (the second-trust deed) and the CRA $6.3 million gap loan (the third-trust deed) remained in place, to be repaid out of surplus cash flow.

*Source:* Thomas Safran & Associates.

# Maple Court, New York City, New York

In the Maple Court development, affordable ownership housing has been developed on an infill site through the formation of a limited-equity cooperative.

Maple Court is a 135-unit, limited-equity cooperative built on a vacant block along Madison Avenue in East Harlem. North General Hospital (NGH), a community health care provider and East Harlem's largest private employer, served as the community sponsor. Sparrow Construction Company developed the project and coordinated the project's planning, construction, marketing, and sales. Other members of the development partnership included Chase Manhattan Bank,

which provided the construction financing; the New York City Housing Development Corporation (HDC); and the New York City Department of Housing Preservation and Development (HPD).

Because limited-equity cooperatives like Maple Court have affordable prices and require little money from the shareholder upfront, they are viewed as one way to make the ownership of multifamily housing units possible for moderate-income households in the city. Through this arrangement, the sharehold purchaser owns shares in the cooperative corporation that actually owns the building; the shareholder can occupy a dwelling unit

by entering into a proprietary lease with the cooperative association.

## The Site

The project was built on a vacant city block bounded by Madison and Park avenues between 122nd and 123rd streets in East Harlem, New York City. It is sited across from Marcus Garvey Park (formerly known as Mount Morris Park) in the Milbank Frawley Circle urban renewal area. The elevated Metro North commuter railroad runs nearby, and the project has easy access to the Lexington Avenue subway station. North General Hospital recently built a new, 240-bed hospital across

Maple Court, a limited-equity, co-operative apartment development in New York City, stands directly across the street from Marcus Garvey Park.

from the Maple Court site on East 122nd Street.

The project is located in a federally designated empowerment zone, in a neighborhood the city code defines as a "targeted area of economic distress." The surrounding area contains numerous lots that were cleared as part of the urban renewal program, some abandoned buildings, and some public and assisted multifamily housing that has been maintained in reasonably good condition. The major commercial corridor serving the district—125th Street—is distressed, and efforts to revitalize it are underway.

## Planning and Permitting

In 1989, when NGH began construction of a new hospital to replace its old facility, hospital officials recognized that it was in their enlightened self-interest to participate actively in strengthening the fabric of the surrounding neighborhood. They built an office annex and outpatient building on a nearby site on Madison Avenue and, to generate development and promote economic diversity within the community, decided to participate in building new, affordable housing in the environs.

NGH conducted informal surveys and focus groups with area residents through church and community meetings to determine the potential market for housing. Responses indicated that many people who had formerly lived in Harlem would return if new homeownership opportunities were available and that some exist-

ing residents were eager to move from subsidized rental housing and from rental housing to homeownership.

Portions of the Maple Court site had been cleared by the city under its urban renewal program. Other portions were city-owned and were transferred to NGH through the city's Uniform Land Use review process. Coordination of city, state, and community efforts took seven years.

After North General Hospital agreed to buy the land, it issued a request for proposals for its development. Sparrow Construction's proposal was chosen because it featured a limited-equity cooperative financed by tax-exempt bonds to make apartments affordable to buyers with limited cash and because its proposed low-rise design was compatible with the surrounding community.

NGH and Sparrow Construction formed a nonprofit subsidiary, Maple Court Housing Development Fund Company, Inc., to take ownership of the site. Actual project development and construction were uneventful. The development proceeded as-of-right under the city's zoning ordinance but required HPD architectural design review.

The development of the Maple Court cooperative has had a positive effect on the neighborhood. Additional private development is underway, the streets are cleaner, and the city is assembling a number of brownstone houses in the area for renovation by private developers and for eventual sale to owner/occupants.

The project's second phase, to be known as Maple Plaza,

is now underway on the block adjacent to Maple Court between 123rd and 124th streets. Also designed as a limited-equity cooperative, the second phase will provide 155 dwelling units—targeted for similar-income households, with an allowance for higher-income households, because less subsidy is involved—and 12,000 square feet of medical office space. The developers are considering a third phase two blocks from Maple Court that also would be a cooperative.

## Design and Construction

The project is a U-shaped, midrise elevator building surrounding a secured, landscaped courtyard. The six-story front of the building faces the park. Two four-story wings, separated by the courtyard, project back along the side streets. The building includes a dramatic lobby and 24-hour concierge service. Native maple trees shade the courtyard, which contains umbrella tables and a play area for children.

The building contains a total of 135 units, including one superintendent's unit. The two- and three-bedroom apartments range in size from 777 to 1,175 square feet—units are larger than the hospital originally conceived—and feature a variety of floor plans. On the first floor, townhouse-style apartments that are entered from the gated courtyard occupy a transverse section of the floor. To ensure privacy and safety for occupants of first-floor units, the developer raised the elevation of the building and installed privacy fencing along the street.

Apartments on the upper floors are entered through the courtyard to the elevator lobby and are arranged along double-loaded corridors. All units include wall-to-wall carpeting, designer kitchens, and tiled bathrooms; many have a terrace or patio. Low fencing defines and protects private patios, and canvas awnings shade balconies on the top floor of the courtyard side.

## Financing

Maple Court's total development cost was $18.2 million. The project received a 30-year, permanent, blanket, below-market-interest first mortgage from the New York City Housing Development Corporation (HDC), with the funds coming from the sale of tax-exempt, qualified mortgage revenue bonds. (The State of New York Mortgage Agency—SONYMA—provided credit enhancement for the bonds by agreeing to insure the HDC permanent mortgage, and Fannie Mae purchased the bonds through a private placement, thus helping to keep transaction costs down.)

The New York City Department of Housing Preservation and Development (HPD) afforded a zero-interest construction loan from the city's capital budget. The loan was converted into a subordinate, zero-interest permanent loan. The development team bought the land from the city, which took back a subordinate purchase-money mortgage for the difference between the cash price and the appraised value of the land. The two HPD mortgages charged no interest, and the loan will be forgiven in 25 years. The HPD loans are repayable only in the form of 50 percent of any profit from appreciation in value when the units are sold. In addition, Maple Court qualified for real estate tax abatements from the city.

The development worked financially in part because the 7,000 square feet of medical office space within the building ensured that a certain amount of the project would be supported by a guaranteed lease with NGH.

## Marketing and Management

The actual sharehold purchase price—including the average pro rata share of the HDC mortgage, the average pro rata share of the HPD mortgage, the shareholder equity, and the HPD

---

# Maple Court Project Data

## Land Use
Site Area: 2 acres
Number of Units: 135
Gross Density: 67.5 units per acre
Medical Office and Storage: 7,020 square feet
Parking Spaces: 83

## Residential Unit Information

| Unit | Number | Average Monthly Charges | Average Square Feet |
|------|--------|-------------------------|---------------------|
| 1-bedroom | 1 | $671 | 585 |
| 2-bedroom | 97[1] | 827 | 825 |
| 3-bedroom | 37 | 970 | 1,104 |

## Development Cost Information

| | Cost | Cost/Unit |
|---|------|-----------|
| Land | $ 1,200,00 | $ 8,889 |
| Hard Costs | 12,330,150 | 91,334 |
| Soft Costs | 4,701,347 | 34,825 |
| Total | $18,231,497 | $135,048 |

## Sources of Permanent Financing

| | Cost | Cost/Unit |
|---|------|-----------|
| New York City Land Lien | $ 1,132,500 | $ 8,389 |
| New York City Assistance Agreement | 4,725,000 | 35,000 |
| Shareholders' Equity | 510,370 | 3,780 |
| HDC Permanent Loan | 11,863,627 | 87,879 |
| Total | $18,231,497 | $135,048 |

1. Includes one superintendent's unit.

subsidies—averaged $136,056, compared with the $206,800 New York City average purchase price for a new single-family house. Downpayments averaged $3,811, within a range of $2,944 to $4,810, amounts comparable to the deposits required for rental units. Buyers did not have to obtain mortgage financing because the mortgages are included in their monthly maintenance charges, which average $865 per month, And the tenant/shareholder is entitled to a tax deduction of the mortgage interest.

Forty percent of the units were allocated for existing neighborhood residents; in fact, more than 60 percent of residents came from within the community.

Marketing was done by a private firm hired by the developer. The project was advertised through the newspaper and at community meetings arranged by the hospital. Potential purchasers were selected by lottery because the number of applicants greatly outnumbered the units available, and applicants had to meet income restrictions to qualify for project financing. Based on the area median incomes, the target market was households with incomes of between $27,000 and $60,000.

Shareholders are required to use the units as their primary residences, no subletting is allowed, and restrictions limit resale prices for shares in the co-operative to 110 percent of the New York City median purchase price for existing housing. Resale restrictions will apply for at least 30 years. Tenant/shareholders are required to pay the city a portion of any profits gained from the sales of their shares in the cooperative corporation.

When the development had been completed and the residents were in place, a board of directors, consisting of project shareholders, was appointed to assume control of the project.

## Experience Gained

- Based on the experience at Maple Court, the second-phase building will be higher and H-shaped to make more of an entryway and to avoid a massive-looking exterior and long interior corridors. The lobby will be more efficient, more units will have balconies, and the top two floors will be designed as "penthouse" floors.

- Putting together a financial structure with different agencies and different sources requires considerable time, patience, and flexibility.

- The sales structure of the limited-equity cooperative concept benefited both the developers and the buyers: it made the units affordable; buyers did not need to locate their own financing; there was no waiting to get loans; it was simpler to qualify applicants; and closings were done en masse.

- According to HDC's Barbara Udell, an infill development such as Maple Court has a much better chance of moving forward if it involves a major sponsor, such as a hospital or university, that has a long-term stake in the community.

- The development has proved that there is a market for moderate-income housing in the area and that a more diverse economic mix can be attracted to live—and remain—in inner-city areas if offered the right product at the right price.

*Source: ULI Project Reference File* report, Volume 27, Number 2.

# Meacham Park, Kirkwood, Missouri

The Meacham Park development demonstrates the creative use of tax increment financing (TIF) to finance infill housing development and neighborhood revitalization. The DESCO Group of St. Louis, in conjunction with the city of Kirkwood, Missouri, plans to revitalize one of the most economically depressed neighborhoods in St. Louis County through financing made possible by the development of a major regional shopping center. The project will result in new affordable infill housing, as well as in the renovation of existing houses in Kirkwood's Meacham Park neighborhood.

DESCO intends to develop Kirkwood Commons Shopping Center, a $52 million, 522,500-square-foot power center on the eastern third of Meacham Park. Key to the developer's plan is the use of $21 million in tax increment financing (TIF), which typically involves the issuance of bonds to make infrastructure improvements for developments that otherwise would not be financially feasible. The additional real estate taxes and nearly one-half of the sales taxes generated by Kirkwood Commons will be used to pay off the TIF debt.

About $4 million from the TIF is earmarked for new housing, housing renovation, infrastructure, and other improvements in Meacham Park, and the remaining $17 million will facilitate the development of Kirkwood Commons. Many of the neighborhood improve-

The St. Louis Housing Authority is spending an average of $13,000 per property to renovate its single-family houses in Meacham Park. Monies from tax increment financing will be used to renovate other neighborhood homes.

ments will occur while the shopping center is under construction. The project is the first in the St. Louis area in which TIF money will be used for both residential and commercial redevelopment.

Meacham Park is one of the oldest settlements in St. Louis County. The houses consist mainly of small bungalows built

over the past 50 years, often with minimal construction standards. The median price of a house in the project area is $32,000, in contrast to $71,311 in the St. Louis region, $83,500 in St. Louis County, and $100,500 in Kirkwood. The area has some 1,000 primarily minority residents and nearly 350 housing units, one-third of which are

103

considered deteriorated or dilapidated by city standards. Nearly 10 percent of the housing is vacant, and the neighborhood is dotted with vacant lots.

The goals of the residential rehabilitation effort are to bring existing property up to city codes, to improve property values, to subsidize single-family lots, and to provide an incentive for current renters to buy homes.

DESCO will develop 55 acres of the 135-acre redevelopment area for Kirkwood Commons. Construction of the shopping center, which was scheduled to begin in mid-1997, is expected to generate an estimated $153 million in annual sales. A projected $2.6 million will be available annually to pay off

the TIF, and DESCO will secure private financing to fund costs beyond those eligible for tax increment financing.

Improvements to the remaining residential portion of Meacham Park will include the construction of new homes; grants of up to $15,000 to existing homeowners to renovate their properties; landscaping; street improvements; and development of a new park. Funding for the improvements will come from several sources, primarily tax increment financing.

Under DESCO's redevelopment plan, 65 vacant lots in the residential neighborhood will be acquired for 27 new housing-authority houses. Tenants in the existing houses will be able to rent the new homes at their

current monthly lease rate or will be given the opportunity to buy them from the housing authority. The St. Louis County Housing Authority is also renovating its 35 single-family properties in the residential redevelopment area. Tenants in these houses are being given a chance to buy the homes from the housing authority with no downpayment. In addition, DESCO will construct an affordable new home in the residential redevelopment area for any existing owner/occupant in the commercial buyout area who wishes to stay in Meacham Park.

*Source:* Excerpted from Joseph A. Maloney, "Revitalizing an Ailing Suburban Neighborhood," *Urban Land* (April 1997).

## Chapter Notes

1. New York City Housing Partnership, *Building in Partnership: A Blueprint for Urban Housing Programs* (November 1994), p. 23.

2. Example provided by Local Government Commission, Sacramento, California.

3. Nancy Bragado, Judy Corbett, and Sharon Sprowls, *Building Livable Communities: A Policymaker's Guide to Infill Development* (Washington, D.C.: Center for Livable Communities and Local Government Commission, 1995), p. 8.

4. New York City Housing Partnership, *Building in Partnership*, pp. 50–51.

5. This section is excerpted from Susan Hobart and Robert Schwartz, *Financing Multifamily Housing Using Section 42 Low-Income Housing Tax Credits*, ULI Working Paper 654 (August 1996).

6. William F. Delvac, Susan Escherich, and Bridget Hartman, *Affordable Housing through Historic Preservation* (Washington, D.C.: U.S. Department of the Interior, National Park Service, no publication date given), p. 9.

7. Susan Escherich, "Mercy Family Plaza," in Delvac et al., *Affordable Housing through Historic Preservation*, p. 44.

## CHAPTER 6

# How Local Governments Can Help

*The Local Government Commission, Sacramento, California, contributed to this chapter.*

**C**ities have a wide variety of resources and tools at their disposal with which to encourage infill housing development in older neighborhoods. Besides entering into public/private financing partnerships, they can establish a planning and regulatory framework that encourages infill housing development, make public investments in targeted communities, and provide various other kinds of assistance to infill housing projects. They can stimulate developers' interest in desired infill developments through meetings with developers individually or in groups, through publicly assisted demonstration projects that verify market demand, and through design competitions that award the winning teams attractive packages of development incentives.

Perhaps most important, cities can develop clear visions of what they want their future to hold, write plans to implement these visions, and muster the will to uphold the plans over the long term. Success will largely depend upon strong leaders and a solid citizen participation process that develops a constituency of residents, businesspeople, and interest groups willing to work to monitor and implement policies in the long run.

## Ten Suggested Measures

Following are some of the specific approaches that local governments can use to encourage infill housing development in inner-city neighborhoods.

### 1. Create a planning framework that encourages infill development.

- Through the planning process, a city can identify specific infill sites and can target districts where infill should occur, for example, areas around existing and proposed transit centers. Once these places have been identified, the city should help define a vision for the community, indicating the types of desired development that it is willing to assist.
- Planning for targeted areas should include a specific plan for infill locations and design guidelines for development and rehabilitation in these locations.
- The city must be prepared to address comprehensively the various needs of the neighborhoods designated for infill development. New housing development, especially in older, declining neighborhoods, cannot succeed in isolation. For infill development to work, neighborhoods must be improved through a strategy that includes the creation of jobs, retail development, improved transportation, community-based policing, coordinated social services, a streamlined regulatory process, community participation, and an aggressive marketing campaign.
- The city planning department must collaborate with other agencies whose activities are affected by infill development (transit agencies, school districts, service providers, and so on) and must encourage joint development.

## Examples

*Targeting of sites for infill development.* The city of Chico, California, recently adopted a general plan that contains a wide range of policies and recommendations that designate sites for infill development and that create "neighborhoods, not subdivisions." One high-priority infill site identified by the plan is the Diamond Match site. Through the plan, the city's intentions are to minimize development pressure on agricultural lands and to promote lively activity centers in town.

*Use of specific plans.* The city of San Jose, California, has adopted as part of its general plan a housing initiative calling for intensification of housing along transit corridors and in other specified areas. The city has prepared a number of specific plans to implement these strategies.

One of the first was the Jackson-Taylor Residential Strategy. Located four blocks from a light-rail station and one mile from the downtown, this neighborhood is an old industrial warehouse district with a number of vacant or abandoned buildings. The specific plan, adopted in 1991, dictates a transition to walkable, mixed-use neighborhoods containing residences, offices, ground-floor retail, industrial uses, and a daycare center. The city has specified the kinds of uses appropriate for the retail space, including services that allow local residents to satisfy their daily needs within the neighborhood.

*Source:* The Local Government Commission, Sacramento, California.

## 2. Review the regulatory framework—the zoning ordinance, development regulations, building codes, and so forth—to ensure that it encourages rather than discourages the desired new infill housing.

- Development standards must be flexible to allow the development of the irregular, small, or otherwise substandard parcels typical of many older neighborhoods.
- Cities should allow the development of a mix of uses at infill locations and at densities that are sufficient to make infill development economically feasible.
- Local governments can offer density bonuses for housing developments that fulfill certain public goals, such as infill housing development projects.
- Localities should be flexible in interpreting building codes and should consider enacting rehabilitation codes to encourage the renovation of usable existing buildings.

- The city can also encourage infill development through the regulatory framework by waiving development fees for sewers, parks, schools, and so on, or by reducing or delaying development fees until the developer sees a positive cash flow.
- Cities can also reduce the number of parking spaces required for developments in which people can walk or take public transportation to their jobs, and they can adjust "level-of-service" street standards for infill projects that promote alternatives to automobile use.
- Development fees can be structured to encourage infill and discourage sprawl, for example, through a surcharge calculated according to the distance from the city core.
- Cities should consider amending their zoning ordinances to allow the installation on infill parcels of manufactured houses meeting the design guidelines for the neighborhood.

The guiding principle for cities in their review of the regulatory framework is to avoid over-regulating weak development environments; instead, they should encourage development with incentives.

Cities can also use their regulatory powers to discourage certain kinds of private sector decisions and actions in targeted neighborhoods. For example, in neighborhoods where speculation in land or properties makes the cost of revitalization prohibitive, "the city may need to employ more aggressive code enforcement, use of its urban renewal condemnation powers, and/or some form of speculator tax to encourage redevelopment."[1]

## Examples

*Revised zoning codes.* The city of San Diego is undergoing a comprehensive zoning code update to improve the effectiveness of the city's regulations and to streamline permit processing. A major goal of the code update is to increase certainty in the permit process by providing objective regulations that can be reviewed at a staff level. The code update addresses such infill issues as residential design standards, shared parking, landscaping, and nonconforming rights.

In addition, several of the proposed amendments have been drafted to implement the city's Transit-Oriented Development (TOD) Design Guidelines (adopted in 1992), including: pedestrian-oriented commercial zones, mixed-use incentives, reduced parking requirements along

By developing the Falconer, an eight-unit, multifamily cooperative housing development, Heartland Properties, Inc., the city of Madison, and Common Wealth Development created high-quality affordable housing for residents of inner-city Madison, Wisconsin.

transit corridors, a townhouse zone, a small-lot single-family zone that addresses garage placement, and a new "urban village" zone.

*Use of impact fees.* The city of Lancaster, California, has adopted an Urban Structure Program that discourages urban sprawl by adding operations costs to its development impact fee. The impact fee specifies an operations fee that includes a 2 percent surcharge (over a fee charged for capital improvements) for each mile that a project is located outside of the city's core. The fee assumes a 20-year operations life span. The program is based on a fiscal analysis of the costs of providing distance-related public services, like street sweeping and community safety.

*Regulatory flexibility and incentives.* The city of Sacramento offers developers the option to use "infill site" regulations that provide more flexibility than standard city zoning and that offer incentives to infill development.

The St. Francis housing project, a 48-unit senior and family housing complex, benefited from the infill incentives. The project was developed as a joint venture between the Catholic diocese and a local nonprofit housing corporation. The project used a 25 percent density bonus over the permitted zoning and paid no city water development fees. Initial controversy surrounding this project

was removed when the applicants worked closely with parents of the children attending the neighboring school and the local neighborhood association to redesign the project, so that its massing and scale would be more sensitive to the existing neighborhood.

*Source:* The Local Government Commission, Sacramento, California.

### 3. Facilitate the process and lower the costs of infill development by providing high-priority processing of development approvals and permits to infill developers.

- Cities and other local governments can define a separate review process for infill development and/or assign people to assist infill developers in identifying and negotiating the required approvals.
- They can also take steps to make the approval process more efficient and more certain, for example, by designating "by-right zones" in which cities must issue the appropriate permit if the project meets specified requirements.
- They can establish thresholds under which smaller projects can be rapidly permitted, saving extensive reviews for larger developments and environmentally sensitive sites.

- They can use self-certification to ensure—and speed up—compliance with regulatory requirements. Under self-certification, contractors assume responsibility for inspecting and certifying the correct completion of their own work. Quality is assured by random spot checks; contractors who cheat lose their licenses.

- Localities can grant waivers to enable more flexibility in design and development. For instance, during the approvals process for Summit Place, an award-winning infill development with mixed housing types, the city of St. Paul, Minnesota, granted developer Robert Engstrom 27 variances for such items as height limits, front- and sideyard setbacks, density, percent coverage of lots and lot lines, rear-access garages, and vacating of the existing alleys.[2]

  In Columbus, Ohio, the city provided upfront all of the necessary approvals and variances on 47 single-family units that were developed on scattered vacant lots as part of the Renaissance development, a neighborhood revitalization project involving the rehabilitation and new construction of some 500 structures.

- Local jurisdictions can prepare master environmental impact reports, enabling conforming projects to proceed without another environmental review.

- And they can consolidate reviews to minimize the numbers and amounts of required fees and permits.

### Examples

*Fast-track permitting.* Fast-track permitting benefited the developers of San Diego's uptown district. In November 1987, the city of San Diego issued a request for proposals for the site of a former Sears store in the Hillcrest neighborhood, a few miles north of downtown San Diego. An exclusive negotiation agreement was entered into in February 1988, followed by hearings in May 1988 and the close of escrow in June of that year. Construction was complete by the end of 1989. This highly successful project contains 320 housing units, a 42,500-square-foot grocery store with underground parking, an additional 94,500 square feet of commercial space, and a 3,000-square-foot community center.

*Streamlined approval process.* A mayoral task force of building and land development experts in the city of Los Angeles has released a report with recommendations for permit streamlining.

The Ninth Square development has transformed streetscapes in its New Haven, Connecticut, neighborhood.

Three critical areas of reform were identified: (1) streamlining the permit and entitlement process; (2) making the process more predictable; and (3) achieving fairness in fees and exactions. Some of the report's recommendations are:

- Appoint case managers to help applicants through the system.
- Consolidate the permit processes.
- Waive or reduce fees for projects that benefit the public, such as affordable housing.
- Reduce the number of changes to previously approved plans.
- Stop the issuance of conflicting requirements by city employees from different agencies.
- Hold a single public hearing for all approvals.
- Streamline the environmental review process.

Many of the administrative recommendations have already been implemented or are in the process of being implemented through the mayor's directives. Other recommendations are working their way through the ordinance amendment process.

*Source:* The Local Government Commission, Sacramento, California.

## 4. Make public investments and provide public services in neighborhoods targeted for infill development.

In many city infill locations, the need is to build neighborhoods, not just housing. Infill development must be coupled with strategies to encourage reinvestment by existing residents and owners. Homeowners may need incentives to invest in the repair, upkeep, and/or modernization of their own properties. Renters can be encouraged and enabled to purchase houses in the community.

The city can invest directly in upgrading the neighborhood, the property, and the infrastructure. It can use public facilities and publicly sponsored developments and amenities to attract investment by locating them in places where infill development is desired. In particular, it can address potential problems with aging and the capacity of affected roadways and sewer and water systems before encouraging infill. In the eyes of at least one observer, the provision of needed public services is "the most valuable in-kind service cities can provide," and this includes keeping vacant properties clean and unblighted and improving both the reality and the image of areas targeted for infill development.[3]

Cities must also make certain that they deliver public services well to areas targeted for infill development. Services such as police protection, public education, road repair and maintenance, trash collection, code enforcement, demolition of blighted vacant structures, maintenance of vacant lots, street lighting and landscaping, and provision of recreational facilities and programming can help make urban neighborhoods attractive for private investment.

### *Example*

*Provision of public services.* The city of Pasadena, California, has launched an ambitious partnership to enhance city services across the board for a neighborhood that had been slated for demolition before an infill strategy was pursued. Working with local businesses and residents, the city established a neighborhood community policing unit, improved code enforcement and street cleaning, organized a neighborhood improvement association, targeted home rehabilitation loans to the area, cosponsored an annual volunteer cleanup effort using citywide resources, and helped developers to build nearly a dozen residential and commercial infill projects. The Lincoln Triangle neighborhood revitalization effort turned around the neighborhood, making it a desirable place for private investment and increasing property values.

*Source:* The Local Government Commission, Sacramento, California.

## 5. Provide potential developers with valuable information.

A city can prepare and disseminate a current and accurate inventory of vacant land parcels. Such an inventory should identify city-owned properties and properties with known environmental concerns. At the same time, the city can provide prospective developers with information on the city's priorities for development and on the kinds of incentives and assistance it can make available to encourage the desired development.

## 6. Prepare master environmental impact reports.

Master environmental impact reports (EIRs) can be used to assess the impacts and determine the mitigation measures needed for building a redevelopment plan, specific plan, or community plan. Later, proposed projects that implement the plan may not have to conduct additional environmental reviews or at least may be required only to focus on a few identified issues. The costs for the master EIR may still be recouped through project development fees but, because of economies of scale and the shorter permitting time required, may cost developers less than if full EIRs were required for each project.

Master EIRs can also be used for policy or regulatory changes. For example, if a community adopts policies and amends its zoning code to allow mixed-use development, a master EIR can be prepared that analyzes the impacts of the policy and zoning code changes and that recommends mitigation measures. Any projects that comply with the regulations and are allowed under the new policies can then proceed without another environmental review.

### 7. Assist infill developers with land acquisition and assembly.

Cities can assist developers with land acquisition by making available at little or no cost foreclosed properties or other publicly owned lands in neighborhoods targeted for infill development. They can discourage land speculation by taxing vacant land at higher rates. Cities can use their power of eminent domain to help assemble several lots for an infill project. In many places, cities can bank land to help assemble parcels whose taxes are delinquent. And localities might also consider initiating the development of surplus public lands as a joint venture with private developers.

To develop a specific infill site, cities can offer city-owned land to developers who agree to build appropriate infill projects there, or can swap city-owned property for developer-owned parcels. For example, the owner of a key property in a district targeted for infill development who is unwilling to build on that site may be willing to accept in exchange a city-owned parcel of similar value, allowing the city to move forward on the targeted site. Many cities own property acquired through tax foreclosure or through a public use condemnation action for a park, street, school, or other facility that was not built. Thorough inventorying of these sites may yield opportunities for exchanges or contributions to projects that can significantly lower the projects' costs.

### Example
*Provision of land.* In Boston, the city is acquiring 747 infill properties—mostly city-owned—and designating them for housing development in the so-called Project 747. Developers are invited to

bid on the properties. Selection is based not only on the dollar amount of the bid but also on the quality of the design, the developer's track record, and the preferences of neighborhood residents. The financing package for the development projects comes from Community Development Block Grants, the Massachusetts Housing Finance Authority, the Boston linkage program, and local banks.[4]

In another example, the Norfolk Redevelopment Housing Authority, by assuming a significant portion of the risk through provision of land, made it possible for The Christopher Companies of McLean, Virginia, to develop Freemason Harbour, a condominium project that resulted from the rebuilding of an old cotton warehouse on the Elizabeth River near the Ghent Square redevelopment area of Norfolk. The housing authority assembled the land and accepted a low downpayment from the developer, who paid the remainder of the price of the land as each condominium unit was sold. The developer never owned the land: the housing authority and the developer jointly signed the owners' deeds at the time of purchase. In addition, the housing authority subordinated its interest to the construction loan. According to Fred Kober, president of The Christopher Companies, the advantage to his firm was that it did not have to carry a land loan, and an advantage to the housing authority—in addition to enabling a needed project to go forward—was that, because it kept control of the land, it knew the project would be completed.

Thomas Safran, a Los Angeles developer of affordable housing, adds that local governments also have the power to close or reroute streets and alleys to enable the consolidation of land parcels as part of a land assembly effort.

### 8. Gain community acceptance for infill housing projects by:
- Educating the community about the public benefits of infill and the tradeoffs between infill development and sprawl, and disseminating factual information on higher-density and affordable housing.
- Establishing strong, written policy statements that developers can use to support the approval of controversial infill projects.
- Helping to resolve conflicts between builders and local interest groups.
- Working with environmentalists and transit advocates to gain support for infill housing.

## Example

*Assuring good design quality.* King County, Washington, officials started the Quality Urban Environment Project to identify methods of working with developers and communities to improve the design and quality of new construction, resulting in better community acceptance of higher densities. The Project is also reviewing codes and procedures to make sure that the development review process matches the overall vision for what new development should look like.

A demonstration area has been designated in two square miles just outside Seattle. Specific ideas that will be tested there include ways to give residents earlier, more meaningful opportunities for input in the review and design of new construction; ways to include and fund amenities; incentives to encourage needed kinds of development; and improvements to the permit system. A primary goal of the Project is to find ways to serve community needs without increasing the time and cost required for the development review process.

*Source:* The Local Government Commission, Sacramento, California.

## 9. Help individual projects succeed by:

- Leasing space in new projects for city/county offices.
- Lending city staff to projects.
- Assisting in relocating existing residents, for example, by providing Section 8 certificates and relocation funds.
- Helping with funding applications.
- Sharing studies and market information.

## Example

*Marketing study.* Because existing marketing studies generally focus on the single-family house in the suburbs, the Seattle Planning Department and the Puget Sound Regional Council undertook their own marketing study to "determine how people can be attracted to reside in dense central cities in general and 'urban villages' in Seattle in particular." They found that 79 percent of the respondents preferred a single-family house over any other type of residence. Twenty-seven percent, however, said they would be willing to live in higher-density housing if it provided the chance to own their own homes, 18 percent more if it offered the various advantages of living near city centers, and 17 percent more if there were lower crime rates and higher school quality.

*Source:* The Local Government Commission, Sacramento, California.

## 10. Consider creative institutional solutions.

When a city wants to encourage a large-scale, long-term, and inherently high-risk infill housing development, it must recognize that "the public sector lacks the flexibility in negotiations and contracting that is required to undertake such projects and attract developers."[5] A public/private entity should be created to identify and initiate projects and to maintain momentum.

For example, East Pointe Commons, a low-rise, 600-unit market-rate rental and for-sale housing development and retail center a few blocks from downtown Milwaukee, was facilitated by the Milwaukee Redevelopment Corporation, a private, civic-oriented corporation that was able to coordinate the various actors and shepherd the effort to successful realization after years of intragovernmental haggling.

This view of the Social Hall, looking west, highlights the extensive masonry restoration work done for Mercy Family Plaza in San Francisco.

# Strategies and Incentives for Public Assistance

## Strategies for Enhancing the Risk/Return Relationship of Private Investment
- Reduce capital costs
- Absorb demands for new or improved infrastructure
- Lower operating costs
- Increase opportunity for development
- Reduce debt service burden
- Reduce predevelopment risk
- Enhance availability of private capital

## Direct Financial Assistance

*Land Assembly*
- Acquisition
- Demolition
- Relocation
- Writedowns

*Capital Improvements*
- Infrastructure
- Parking garages
- Open space and amenities
- Programmatic facilities

*Grant Assistance*
- Cost sharing of private improvements
- Payment for predevelopment studies

*Debt Financing*
- Direct loans
- Below-market interest rates
- Loan guarantees
- Credit enhancements

## Indirect Assistance
- Zoning or density bonuses
- Transfers of development rights
- Transfers of air rights
- Regulatory relief from zoning and building codes
- Reduced processing time for project approvals
- Quick take by eminent domain
- Design coordination in public/private projects
- Below-cost utilities, if publicly owned
- Arbitration of disputes that might arise
- Government commitments to rent space

## Financing Strategies
*Intergovernmental Grants*
- Community Development Block Grants
- Section 108 guaranteed loans
- State economic development grants

*Local Debt Financing*
- General obligation bonds
- Revenue bonds
- Industrial development bonds

*Off-Budget Financing*
- Lease-purchase agreements
- Ground leases
- Land/building swaps
- Property tax abatements

*Dedicated Sources of Local Funds*
- Special district assessments
- Tax increment financing
- Earmarked sales or special-purpose taxes
- Reuse of UDAG loan paybacks

*General Budget Revenues*

*Source:* Mike E. Miles, Richard L. Haney, and Gayle Berens, *Real Estate Development: Principles and Process,* Second Edition (Washington, D.C.: Urban Land Institute, 1996), p. 279.

# Conclusion

Developers are turning to infill housing as a potential market niche at a time when development opportunities in other locations have become saturated or overly competitive. Infill housing development can be challenging, but for the developer with strong entrepreneurial skills, with access to financing, and with a willing partner in city government, infill housing can also be rewarding. Studies in city after city continue to demonstrate not only the need for affordable housing but also the existence of sizable markets for rental and for-sale housing in inner-city locations. "Infill housing and mixed-use development offer some of the most creative and profitable opportunities in development today."[6]

The successful development of infill housing offers other rewards as well. From a city's point of view, and from the point of view of the larger metropolitan community, such developments can help engender confidence in a community's future, stimulate additional investment, and help restore vitality to the central city.

# Quality Hill, Kansas City, Missouri

The Quality Hill urban revitalization project is a good example of how public/private leadership and cooperation have changed a blighted area into a viable downtown neighborhood, sparked the redevelopment of adjacent areas, and brought people back to the city to live as well as work.

The Quality Hill project provides mixed-income housing through the restoration of old structures and construction of new ones. The development, on the western edge of downtown Kansas City, Missouri, is part of a 25-block neighborhood also known as Quality Hill, a deteriorated historic district with origins in the mid-1800s. Work on the project began in 1985 and continues today.

The development has helped revitalize the city, stimulating the development of 800 to 900 additional housing units, retail space, approximately 1 million square feet of new or rehabilitated office space, and 2,800 new parking spaces. In addition, as a result of the new environment and image it has created, Quality Hill has become the location of choice for nonprofit organizations, generating further employment downtown. Among the organizations that have moved to Quality Hill are the American Cancer Society, United Way, Arthritis Foundation, Greater Kansas City Sports Commission, Junior Chamber of Commerce, Brain Injury Association, and Hispanic Economic Development Corporation.

## The Site

Quality Hill is an infill project occupying 8.5 acres and consisting of ten new buildings, 13 renovated ones, and two above-ground parking structures. The redevelopment site occupies approximately 20 percent of the historic Quality Hill neighborhood, where there had

been ample evidence of both past neglect and recent renewal: boarded-up houses sat on overgrown lots not far from a new, high-rise office building and a relocated data processing company. Around the site were modest apartment buildings, private houses (some converted into small offices), a high rise with housing for the elderly,

The headquarters building for United Way, part of the multiblock Quality Hill development in Kansas City, Missouri, is shown here before and after rehabilitation.

parking lots, a bar and grill, a few restaurants, and a market with minimal provisions. A historic cathedral with a reflective golden dome is a neighborhood landmark.

In the Victorian era, Quality Hill was an affluent neighborhood of elegant red brick houses and hotels, built by merchants who left New England to find their fortunes. The area began to decline at the turn of the 20th century, when stockyards were built nearby; the odors drove away residents and businesses. The stockyards were removed after World War II, but the deterioration continued. Buildings were used primarily by transient renters and indigents, and many had been damaged by fire and neglect.

There was sporadic development activity during the 1960s, but Quality Hill did not become a serious target for redevelopment until the early 1980s. The area immediately to the east had been rebuilt with a new hotel, a convention center, several theaters, and Allis Park Plaza, a large open space used for entertainment programs. This urban renewal activity and surging commercial construction in the CBD motivated community leaders to consider revitalizing the adjacent residential neighborhood and restoring the dynamics of a 24-hour downtown where people would live and spend their free time as well as work.

## Planning

McCormack Baron & Associates (MBA), Inc., a development company from St. Louis, began planning for Quality Hill in 1982. MBA found obstacles to overcome, including assembling the ground from different property owners, designing new structures that were compatible with the historic buildings, and creating a complex, multilayered financing package.

Property acquisition required case-by-case negotiations. When completed, the city agreed to acquire the properties, to pay relocation expenses for 200 households and 40 small businesses, and to finance public improvements of streets and street amenities. Several owners kept and rehabilitated their own buildings.

After three years of difficult negotiations, the review process was relatively easy. Construction started in 1985. Development progressed from the western edges of the project area to the east; new construction and renovation occurred simultaneously.

Phase I provides 363 units of housing and 64,000 square feet of office and retail spaces. Phase II, completed in 1989, provides 49 affordable housing units, 15 in a new apartment building and 34 in the nearby Cordova Hotel, now restored and converted into apartments. Twenty percent of the rental units in the renovated buildings of Phase I and all the Phase II units were set aside as affordable housing. Subsidies and low-income housing tax credits will keep rents affordable for at least 15 years.

Phase III, which was funded with LIHTCs, consists of 84 garden apartments for low-income households. Construction on the 2.45-acre site of Phase III was completed in 1993, and the apartments are fully occupied. Phase IV, which was in the planning stage at the time of this writing, is envisioned as a mixed-use development with retail uses on the ground floor and market-rate apartments above.

## Design

The first phase of Quality Hill comprises 23 buildings ranging in height from two to five stories. The new low- and mid-rise buildings blend in with restored ones; setbacks, heights, and designs are consistent with those of the historic structures. The dominant architectural material is red brick, embellished on the new townhouses with gray siding and white trim reminiscent of New England, the point of departure for many original settlers.

Thirteen of the buildings are historic restorations. Constructed before 1928, they retain many original details, while new roofs, rebuilt facades, and replaced gables and turrets have returned them to their original appearance. All have new plumbing and wiring. Ten of these buildings have been remodeled for residential use and offer a range of one- and two-bedroom floor plans.

The three other restored buildings have been converted into commercial uses.

Among the 13 historic structures are ten new residential buildings. Three are apartment buildings: two three-story buildings have one-bedroom apartments; one four-story building has three stories of two-bedroom apartments above ground-level retail. Seven of the new structures are groups of attached two-bedroom townhouses, each pair of townhouses having a one-level garden flat built below it.

The city spent over $2 million on streetscape improvements and detailing required by the developer to foster a new neighborhood image: new curbs, gutters, sidewalks, and median strips; street entrances to the neighborhood that have been narrowed to limit through-traffic and marked with large pylons displaying decorative Quality Hill plaques; brick pavers between curbs and sidewalks; brick retaining walls topped with wrought-iron fencing that demarcate property lines; and decorative streetlights and ample street plantings.

## Financing

Development costs of Quality Hill, Phase I, were projected to be $40 million, but the revenues produced by the project would service only $11 million of conventional debt at the tax-exempt bond rate available at the time of closing. The gap of $29 million had to be covered with grants and soft loans. Obtaining financing to fill the gap required more than three years of complex negotiations.

In the pre-1986 tax environment, equity of $11 million came from a limited partnership of individual investors. The offering was managed by the Special Investments Group of Bear, Stearns & Company in New York City. Quality Hill has restored buildings eligible for historic tax credits and affordable dwelling units eligible for low-income housing credits; these credits were incentives

for investors. MBA became the managing general partner and maintained 1 percent ownership. The principal landowner was paid one-eighth of MBA's share in return for his on-site properties.

An additional $4 million was raised from a coalition of 17 Kansas City businesses, banks, and foundations. The city supplied $7.5 million from community development funds and $11 million in first-mortgage revenue bonds. In addition, the city gave low-interest loans at 5 percent and agreed to tax abatements of 100 percent for ten years and 50 percent for the following 15 years.

Financial support from the city and from private sector investors led to relatively quick action on the city's request for federal funds, and Quality Hill received an Urban Development Action Grant (UDAG) of $6.55 million.

The closing took ten days and nights to complete. The complex negotiations resulted in the following alignment: the first-mortgage lender is a local bank; the Hall Family Foundation is in the secondary mortgage position; UDAG is in the third mortgage position; and there are equity partners. Payback comes mostly from property sales. Redistribution occurs in various ways: mortgage writedowns, reinvestment in the area, and funds made available to minority groups.

In addition to equity, MBA receives a developer's consultant fee upfront and an annual management fee of 5 percent of the gross rents.

As of December 1996, McCormack Baron had repaid

the community loan down to $2.3 million by selling some of the renovated properties and by refinancing the first-mortgage revenue bonds.

## Marketing and Management

Leasing began in 1987. Redevelopment had changed the public perception of the area, and lease-up went quickly. Most renters, who are single people or young marrieds with no children, work downtown.

Security is not a major concern. Still, apartment buildings have secured common entries, and all first-floor and garden apartments have a security system. Parking lots have controlled gate access and good lighting. A security guard patrols at night. Maintenance crews keep streets and sidewalks clean and make building repairs.

## Experience Gained

- In multiparticipant deals, each group should designate a single advocate or spokesperson. These advocates can streamline negotiations by becoming the decision-making group.
- A market niche exists for middle-income downtown housing, but without subsidies, high development costs will drive quality standards below acceptable levels and/or raise rents beyond the reach of the market. Cities then will be left with housing for only the rich and the poor.
- The support of the community establishment is a

## Quality Hill Project Data[1]

### Land Use Information

Site Area: 8.5 acres

Gross Leasable Area: 538,100 square feet

Net Leasable Area: 402,200 square feet

| Property | Number of Structures | Number of Dwelling Units | Residential (Square Feet) | Commercial (Square Feet) |
|---|---|---|---|---|
| Historic Rehabili- tation | 13 | 207 | 186,000 | 45,600 |
| New Construc- tion | 10 | 156[2] | 163,800 | 6,800 |
| Total | 23 | 363 | 349,800 | 52,400 |

### Land Use Plan

| | Size (Square Feet) | Percent of Site |
|---|---|---|
| Residential | 474,000 | 88 |
| Office | 55,600 | 10 |
| Retail | 8,500 | 2 |
| Total | 538,100 | 100 |

### Parking

| | |
|---|---|
| Garage Spaces | 401[3] |
| Lot Spaces | 164 |
| Total | 565[4] |

1. Phase I only.

2. Includes 126 rentals and 30 condominiums.

3. There are two three-level, above-ground parking structures—one with 185 spaces, one with 216 spaces.

4. Each dwelling unit has one free parking space.

5. Includes concrete, masonry, steel, carpentry, waterproofing/roofing, doors/windows.

### Development Cost Information

| | Amount | Percent of Total |
|---|---|---|
| Site Acquisition | $5,500,000 | 13 |
| Site Improvement/Construction | | |
|   General conditions | $3,333,236 | |
|   Demolition/excavation | 1,051,079 | |
|   Construction[5] | 8,455,218 | |
|   Finishes | 4,259,135 | |
|   Specialties, cabinets, equipment, appliances | 2,666,679 | |
|   HVAC | 681,462 | |
|   Plumbing/sewers | 1,296,259 | |
|   Fire protection | 259,252 | |
|   Electrical | 1,917,580 | |
|   Elevators | 209,624 | |
|   Landscaping | 222,216 | |
|   Swimming pool | 37,036 | |
|   Parking garages | 1,703,654 | |
|   Total | $26,092,430 | 70 |
| Public Improvements | $ 2,000,000 | |
| Total Soft Costs | $ 6,757,570 | 17 |
| Total Development Costs | $40,350,000 | 100 |

### Sources of Development Funds

| | Amount | Percent of Total |
|---|---|---|
| Equity | $11,000,000 | 27 |
| First-Mortgage Revenue Bonds | 11,000,000 | 27 |
| Community Consortium Loans | 4,000,000 | 10 |
| Urban Development Action Grant | 6,500,000 | 16 |
| CDBG | 350,000 | 1 |
| Site Acquisition (city) | 5,500,000 | 14 |
| Public Improvements (city) | 2,000,000 | 5 |
| Total Sources | $40,350,000 | 100 |

distinct advantage to redevelopment projects in generating the necessary financial resources. Local foundations can be sources of significant financing for central-city developments that have a social purpose.

■ The logic of the Quality Hill project was a primary attraction to investors: the development had defined borders, could produce something unique that would affect a large part of the downtown significantly, and had an identifiable blight problem that could be corrected in a relatively short time.

■ Historic renovation of the older buildings was more costly and time-consuming than anticipated. Thorough investigation of restoration expenses is essential when considering renewal.

*Source:* Excerpted from *ULI Project Reference File* report, Volume 20, Number 16.

# Trinity Court, Yonkers, New York

Trinity Court is an example of a public/private affordable housing initiative undertaken by a private developer, Trinity Development Associates, and the city of Yonkers, New York. The development illustrates the coordination of the actions of municipal and nonprofit agencies and of the developer, the successful use of multiple funding sources, and the value of input from prospective homeowners and the local community.

The project provides affordable homeownership opportunities to first-time homebuyers who live or work in Yonkers. At the same time, the attractive design and the stabilizing presence of owner-occupied units are intended to enhance and revitalize an inner-city community. The project consists of 30 two- and three-bedroom townhouse units clustered in five groups and sited on a 1.5-acre parcel. The units are of modular construction, assembled and finished on site. The use of modular units and limited general amenities has helped hold down construction costs and, thus, sale prices.

## The Site

Trinity Court is located in southwest Yonkers's Hollow section, which contained industrial and residential uses. In the early 1970s, the Yonkers Community Development Agency (CDA) acquired the site as part of its urban renewal plan and cleared the site of its existing, deteriorated buildings.

Traditional styling details such as bay windows, corniced doorways, shutters, and lampposts enhance the modular construction of Trinity Court's townhouses.

The site is surrounded by varying uses that typify a transitional inner-city neighborhood, a vacant parochial school, parks, a senior citizens' housing project, vacant land, and a creek with several high-rise apartment buildings on its opposite bank. The neighborhood is characterized by its tenement rowhouses and its three churches, which are a unifying physical and social presence.

## Development Process and Financing

The development process was begun in December 1988, when Trinity Development Associates submitted to the city an unsolicited housing proposal for the site. Because the site was designated for commercial use under the original urban renewal plan, the city had to rewrite the plan for residential use and obtain state approval

for the change. In addition, the city had to grant use and setback variances to build townhouses.

During the review process, a number of municipal agencies provided design assistance, site planning, and infrastructure assessment. Final approval of the project and the developer's control of the site came with the signing of a land disposition agreement in May 1990. The developer paid the CDA $33,891 (approximately $1,130 per unit) for the land, while the CDA agreed to write down the remaining $330,000 appraised value of the land. The CDA's land writedown took the form of an $11,000 grant issued to each homebuyer to cover the cost of each unit's land. This grant is fully forgiven after ten years of owner-occupancy: if an owner sells a unit in years 1 through 6, the full amount must be paid back at closing; in years 7 through 10, the amount is forgiven at the rate of 25 percent per year.

The Housing Action Council, a not-for-profit housing advocacy group that acts as a conduit for state funds, secured a $750,000 grant from the New York State Affordable Housing Corporation and used it to lower each unit price by $25,000. This arrangement is a nonperforming mortgage, with no payments or interest; it, too, is forgivable after ten years of owner-occupancy, with a sliding payback scale if a unit is sold earlier.

The Westchester County Housing Implementation Fund provided $445,000 to the city for needed infrastructure improvements, including street paving, curbs, utilities, and lights. Finally, the city provided tax abatements authorized by the New York State Economic Development Zone (EDZ) program, which assesses real estate taxes for the first six years based on the unimproved value of each building lot.

## Planning and Design

Originally, the developer's site plan proposed that the 30 townhouses be arranged around a stub-end cul-de-sac, but the city criticized the plan for its layout and its series of "gang parking" pods for six to seven cars each. The city's planning bureau worked with the developer to modify the site plan, changing it into a ring-road concept to establish a better relationship among the residential buildings and to use the land more efficiently. The units thus face each other across the new street to create a close sense of community. Although this arrangement exposes a continuous wall of backyards to the main street and the neighborhood, the effect on the project's surroundings is minimized by the use of rear-wall shutters, soft colors, and landscaping.

Great attention was paid to detailing and landscaping at Trinity Court. While the use of modular housing units was a key to the project's affordability, both the city and the developer were concerned about the bland appearance of the modular box. To impart a sense of style and flavor, roof gables, window boxes, bay windows, cornice-topped doorways, and shutters were added. In addition, the developer voluntarily provided brick facing on scattered units. The overall effects were to break the continuous line of the buildings with interesting details and to give each townhouse a greater impression of individuality.

Foundation plantings around the units soften the base of the housing and, on a practical note, screen utility meter boxes. The streetlights are not today's typical cobra-head issue but a traditional lamppost style. To preserve the architectural and design features, deed restrictions bar owners from modifying a unit's exterior and prohibit raising fences in the yards.

The site's previous use posed an unexpected expense and time delay for the developer, who had to break up and remove the existing, hidden foundations. The developer also bore the additional and unexpected cost of above-standard construction materials, required because of the site's location within one of the city's fire zones: densely developed areas with older, wood-frame structures. Vinyl siding is not allowed here; instead, the units are clad with a costlier, high-gauge aluminum siding.

## Marketing

The sale prices of the townhouses represented a rare opportunity for affordable homeownership in Yonkers, where at that time the median sale price for a single-family house was $232,000. Trinity Court's two-bedroom townhouses sold for $95,000, and its three-bedroom units for $101,000. The townhouses are privately owned as fee-simple units and can be resold at any time on the private market, though little incentive exists to do so because of restrictions that were placed on the resales of units within the first ten years of owner-occupancy to prevent buyer speculation. Eligibility for townhouse purchase was limited to persons or households who lived or worked in Yonkers, who were first-time homebuyers, and who had a combined household income of less than $40,000.

Income qualification proved to be the most difficult hurdle, as many people at the $40,000 income limit had neither an adequate credit history nor enough savings for the 5 percent downpayment. Those who qualified—120 applicants out of a total of some 250—were entered into a lottery to distribute the units, of which 20 percent were reserved for area residents, 40 percent for city residents, and 40 percent for persons employed in the city of Yonkers. Municipal employees represented the largest group of qualifying applicants.

## Experience Gained

- The city's application guidelines for affordable housing, although at first considered by the development team to be onerous and overly detailed, turned out to be useful in planning and anticipating details of the development. Thus, they ultimately speeded up the development process.

- The prequalifying of prospective homebuyers during construction expedited the delivery process. As construction was completed and as certificates of occupancy were obtained, units could simultaneously be closed.
- A variety of funding sources and tax abatement programs can be assembled to minimize development and housing costs.

- Attention to a few architectural details, such as roof gables, window boxes, doorways, and shutters, can help make modular units a viable and attractive option for affordable housing.
- Regular meetings among the developer, neighborhood churches, and area residents encouraged community input and generated support for the project.

## Trinity Court Project Data

### Land Use Information

Site Area: 1.5 acres
Gross Density: 20 dwelling units per acre
Total Dwelling Units: 30
Gross Square Feet: 35,640
Parking Spaces: 40

### Unit Information

| Unit Type | Number Built | Average Size (Square Feet) | Sales Price |
|---|---|---|---|
| 2-bedroom/1.5-bath | 5 | 1,075 | $ 95,000 |
| 3-bedroom/1.5-bath | 25 | 1,275 | 101,000 |

### Development Cost Information

| | Private | Public |
|---|---|---|
| Site Acquisition Cost | $33,891 | $330,000 |
| Site Improvement Costs | | |
| Roadway and parking | | $139,000 |
| Curbs/sidewalks | | 66,000 |
| Sewer/water/drainage | | 180,000 |
| Street lighting | | 40,000 |
| Fees | | 20,000 |
| Total | | $445,000 |

| | Private | Public |
|---|---|---|
| Housing Units' Construction Cost | $2,181,092 | |
| Soft Costs | | |
| Architecture/engineering | $ 55,810 | |
| Project management | 64,125 | |
| Marketing | 17,878 | |
| Legal | 36,390 | |
| Closing costs/taxes/insurance | 165,951 | |
| Construction interest | 85,494 | |
| Security | 35,200 | |
| Developer fee | 113,890 | |
| Other professional costs | 18,060 | |
| Total | $592,798 | |

Total Development Cost: $3,252,781
Average Construction Cost per Unit: $72,703
Average Construction Cost per Gross Square Foot: $61
Average Development Cost per Unit: $108,426
Average Development Cost per Gross Square Foot: $91

*Source:* Excerpted and updated from *ULI Project Reference File* report, Volume 22, Number 9.

### Sources and Uses of Public Funding

| Program | Amount | Use |
|---|---|---|
| Westchester County Housing Implementation Fund | $445,000 | Infrastructure improvements |
| New York State Affordable Housing Corporation | $750,000 | Mortgage defrayal of $25,000 on each unit |
| City Land Disposition Agreement (Yonkers Community Development Agency) | $330,000 | Reduction of land cost, in the form of $11,000 lien on each unit |

# South Williamsburg Homes, Brooklyn, New York

South Williamsburg Homes consists of 105 limited-equity cooperative housing units in 35 three-story, attached buildings that were constructed on city-owned lots scattered through two blocks of Brooklyn in New York City. The project represents a creative adaptation of the New York City Housing Partnership's New Homes Program to meet the needs and concerns of the residents of one of the poorest neighborhoods in the city.

The city and the New York City Housing Partnership started the New Homes Program to address the shortage of affordable homeownership housing in inner-city neighborhoods and the lack of private sector investment there. Through this program, the city provides selected builder/developers with buildable vacant lots, approximately $10,000 per unit in city capital budget funds, and help in securing development approvals. The builder secures private financing and commits to building and selling houses or owner-occupied apartments at a fixed price. The New Homes Program fills with public subsidies the gap between the costs of development and the housing costs that working families can afford; it ensures that as much as 75 percent of development costs are leveraged from private sector sources.

The goals of the South Williamsburg Homes project were to help low-income families establish a stake in their community as new homeowners and to provide a permanent source of decent, affordable housing in a place where much of the housing stock had deteriorated. By filling in a relatively large number of vacant lots scattered over six blocks, the project also sought to encourage housing rehabilitation by current area residents.

## Project Planning

The Williamsburg section of Brooklyn is among the poorest in New York City. The majority of the population is composed of Latinos, African Americans, and Hasidic Jews. The vacant parcels on which the South Williamsburg Homes were built had been eyesores for more than 20 years; strewn with debris and garbage, they were symbols of neighborhood decline. Area residents, as represented by Southside United and Catholic Charities, had long expressed an interest in promoting homeownership on these vacant city-owned parcels and in maximizing the affordability of the units over the long term through the limited-equity cooperative form of ownership.

The South Williamsburg Homes project was the result of the cooperative efforts of the New York City Housing Partnership (through its Housing Partnership Development Corporation, or HPDC), which initiated the development; the city and state of New York, which helped finance it; the Southside United Housing Development Fund Company (also known as Los Sures) and Catholic Charities, which represented the interests of the community and were responsible for marketing the completed units; and H. Randy Lee, a private, for-profit builder who constructed the units.

The lots had been cleared 20 years before but remained undeveloped due to community conflicts over who would be served by a new development on the site.

The scattered-site nature of the project, whose small lots were wedged among existing buildings, complicated the predevelopment process. The builder's experience and the use of modular units enabled him to produce an attractive development within budget and within the projected development schedule.

It took several months for HPDC to terminate leases, demolish structures, clear debris, and provide clean title. A number of unanticipated subsurface complications, such as multiple foundations that required excavation, delayed construction. Additional costs were covered by the contingency fund that had been incorporated into the project's budget.

Construction began on the units in June 1990 and was completed in late 1991, and by the early spring of 1992, the project was entirely occupied.

## Design

The South Williamsburg Homes are attached, three-story, three-unit buildings with masonry facades designed to complement the existing character of the neighborhood. Each full masonry front has six-inch walls that provide insulation for the homes. For security, dead-bolt locks were supplied, and window gates were made available to purchasers. Even though the project is a cooperative, owners were provided with fenced yards for their private use. The bottom and third-floor units have access from the ground floor, while second-floor units are reached via an outdoor spiral staircase.

The units are of modular construction—a cost-saving construction method. Because the time required to build modular units is several months shorter than for site-built housing, the resulting savings in carrying costs include construction-loan interest, insurance, and security costs. In addition, the "hard costs" themselves were approximately $10,000 per unit less than for site-built housing.

There are 70 three-bedroom units and 35 two-bedroom units, with the average size of a three-bedroom unit being 1,210 square feet. Units are of modular, steel-frame construction with facades of masonry. Prefabrication permitted development under the multifamily building code, and one-third of the units were made handicapped-accessible.

## Financing

Construction financing came from four sources. A bank loan covered 50 percent of project costs. The New York City Housing Partnership worked with the builder to engage the Greater New York Savings Bank to originate a $6 million construction loan for which the builder was the borrower and the Partnership the mortgagor. Public subsidies consisted of city capital funds, city funds from the sale of a nearby parcel for market-rate development (cross-subsidy funds), and funds from the state affordable housing corporation.

The land was sold by the city for a cash price of $500 per unit, with the balance of the land value becoming a second lien against the homes. In addition, the builder's equity and deferred fees amounted to some $1.36 million (about $13,000 per unit, or 10 percent of the total cost). The bank required that the builder provide completion and personal payment guarantees.

For permanent financing, the city and state funds converted into a subsidy lien on the project, which declines over 30 years and need not be repaid so long as the cooperative abides by the resale and ownership restrictions. The city's housing development corporation issued tax-exempt mortgage revenue bonds. Proceeds of sale were used to finance the $6.645 million underlying mortgage on the cooperative, which amounted to 95 percent of the appraised value of the property. The tax-exempt financing allowed a low, long-term interest rate of 8.5 percent.

This was the first time that the New York City Housing Partnership had structured the use of mortgage revenue bonds to fund the underlying mortgage on a cooperative. The Partnership worked with the New York State Mortgage Insurance Fund to insure the mortgage, thereby providing the credit enhancement needed to sell the bonds.

In addition, because the land was transferred to a not-for-profit corporation of the New York City Housing Partnership, the project benefited from tax breaks, including exemptions from the mortgage recording tax and the city's real property transfer tax.

## Marketing and Management

Income and sales restrictions were determined by the rules governing mortgages financed by federal single-family mortgage revenue bonds. Units were priced to be affordable to four income groups ranging from $20,000 to $36,000 in annual income, or from 50 to 90 percent of the area median. Average share price was $7,500.

Income and purchase price restrictions remain in place for 30 years, that is, throughout the life of the bonds. At resale, units must be priced to be affordable to families in the same income range (percentage of median income) as the original purchasers, and all purchasers must be owner/occupants. Subsidy funds do not require repayment as long as the cooperative abides by the resale and ownership requirements.

Forty percent of the units have been reserved for local residents. The local sponsor, Southside United, with support from a neighborhood church, did outreach to community residents, while Southside United answered local inquiries on the project, generated qualified local applicants for the units, determined eligibility, and coordinated the sales. Southside is now the managing agent.

## South Williamsburg Homes Project Data

### Uses of Funds

| | |
|---|---:|
| Land Acquisition | $ 52,500 |
| Construction Costs | 9,466,470 |
| Soft Costs | 1,626,061 |
| Financing Fees and Costs | 1,594,015 |
| Total Cost | $12,739,046 |
| Per-Unit Cost | $121,324 |

### Sources of Funds:

**Development Financing**

| | |
|---|---:|
| City Subsidy Funds (0% loan) | $ 1,050,000 |
| Cross-Subsidy Funds (0% loan) | 1,575,000 |
| State Subsidy Funds (recapturable grant) | 2,625,000 |
| Bank Loan | 6,130,735 |
| Builder Equity | 472,500 |
| Builder Fee (funded from sales proceeds) | 885,811 |
| Total | $12,739,046 |

### Permanent Financing

| | |
|---|---:|
| City Subsidy Funds | $1,050,000 |
| | (0% loan) |
| Cross-Subsidy Funds | 1,575,000 |
| | (0% loan) |
| State Subsidy Funds | 2,625,000 |
| | (0% loan) |
| Housing Development Corporation (tax-exempt bond proceeds) | 6,645,000 |
| Purchasers' Downpayments | 844,046 |
| Total | $12,739,046 |

*Source:* New York City Housing Partnership.

## Chapter Notes

1. New York City Housing Partnership, *Building in Partnership: A Blueprint for Urban Housing Programs* (November 1994), p. 23.

2. Nora Richter Greer, "Summit Place: Urban Pioneer in St. Paul," *Urban Land* (April 1993), p. 81.

3. Rick Cole, Nancy Bragado, Judy Corbett, and Sharon Sprowls, "Building Livable Communities New Strategies for Promoting Infill Development," *Urban Land* (September 1996).

4. "Promoting Infill by Removing the Obstacles," *Urban Outlook* (March 30, 1991), p. 6.

5. Harvey Rabinowitz, "Highway to Housing: Milwaukee's East Pointe Commons," *Urban Land* (June 1994), p. 34.

6. Development Strategies, Inc., *Development Strategies Review* (Summer 1992).